SPEAK
INFLUENCE
SELL

WINNING THE HEARTS AND MINDS OF YOUR IDEAL
CUSTOMER THROUGH PUBLIC SPEAKING

ELLIOT KAY

POWERHOUSE
PUBLICATIONS

COPYRIGHT

Powerhouse Publications
www.powerhousepublications.com

TESTIMONIALS

"This is the book to start with on your Public Speaking journey. It's also the book to revisit along your Public Speaking journey. It's packed full of amazing tips – couldn't recommend it enough."

—Charli Hunt,
Founder of Proof Content

"I loved working through *Speak.Grow.Sell*. It's now become my reference handbook, after having initially helped me to bridge the inner conflict I was running between being a busy entrepreneur *and* trying to be a speaker. It provides meaningful insight as well as practical step-by-step guidance on everything that Speaker Express trains on *(attending their courses is my next call to action)*. This book is a meaningful guide on how to powerfully utilise speaking, so that it becomes your most powerful business-growth marketing tool."

—Jenetta Barry,
CEO / Founder - The Epiphany Process

"What's truly surprising about this book is the generosity with which Elliot shares his expertise, garnered from ten years of running Speaker Express and 7,000 hours as a professional speaker and trainer. But, given that his reason for being in business is 'the greater good', maybe it's not surprising at all. The book analyses, in depth and with plenty of examples, the six concepts and practices that are essential for anyone who wants to grow their business through speaking. There is, of course, no substitute for getting up on stage and speaking. One of Elliot's mantras is: "Stage time, of course". However, this book is the best possible starting point."

—Elaine Hopkins,
best-selling Amazon author and speaker (thanks to Elliot)

DEDICATION

To my dearest wife, Emily,
and my wonderful children – may you
always use your voice for good.

Contents

Introduction

Behind every successful influencer lies the power to communicate; the ability to take an idea and connect it in a way that gives your audience a truly powerful, and even life-changing, experience.

Successful and credible leaders today are not only determined by title, background or business, but also by their ability to influence. Nothing influences more than the ability to speak authentically in public, but like most things worth doing, public speaking takes time and effort. To truly master public speaking requires a lifetime of evolution.

Whether you are a business owner looking to pitch for investment, a leader looking to inspire your team, a full-time speaker looking for more significant stage opportunities, or simply have a big vision and are looking to reach like-minded people, the ability to professionally and masterfully speak in public can have a profound effect in growing your business, building your brand, and raising your credibility and influence.

Public speaking is a valuable life skill that's often underdeveloped either because of nerves, simply not knowing where to start, or, in many cases, a lack of speaking experience.

This book is for you whether you already speak or if you are just beginning your journey. I believe it's possible for anyone to use speaking to grow their business and to fall in love with public speaking. It's simply a question of overcoming the fear and eliminating the guesswork. Speaking on stage about your product and brand puts you in a place of power. Speaking is so much more than just dealing with nerves. A part of you already knows that and it's why you're reading this book. My aim is to show you how to succeed as a speaker so that you can focus on the growth of your business and your role as an influencer in your industry.

This concept has been at the heart of Speaker Express, a speaker training company I co-founded, since 2011. It's been the driving force behind the creation of The Speakers' Method, our tried and tested formula that focuses on the six essential areas that drive the success of a business owner who uses public speaking. It's helped thousands of speakers gain more confidence, hone their messaging, significantly increase visibility, and book more gigs to obtain business funding, growth and exposure; all of which are covered in this book.

The Speakers' Method has evolved from a decade of in-depth interviews, research, thousands of consultations, speaking audits, events, workshops and personal experience. This method will help you take the guesswork out of your speaking strategy and enable you to accelerate your speaking ability, no matter where you stand at the moment.

This book is for those of you who are ready to truly play a bigger game using speaking to boost your communication and persuasion so that you become the influencer you know you were meant to be. I'm holding nothing back, because, wherever you are with your public speaking right now, I want to help you move to the next level.

From some of the biggest mistakes to the most stunning successes, I'll be sharing it all, so you can benefit from the knowledge and experience that comes from delivering over 7,000 hours of talks, being an international public speaker for over ten years, and working with thousands of business owners globally.

At the end of some of the chapters, you'll find a summary of takeaways, together with suggested action steps. I recommend getting yourself a notebook where you can jot down any additional ideas you might have. As you read, check in with yourself to see what resonates. There'll be flashes of inspiration, moments of frustration, feelings of triumph, and maybe even a crisis in confidence. Sharing them in your notebook will embed your learning and help you arrive at your authentic and individual strategy to use public speaking in whatever way you want.

Pause and Temperature Check

How are your public speaking abilities right now?

Before reading on, take a minute to think about where you are at right now with your speaking and with your business. Maybe by now your business has grown into a bigger team or maybe you are still a fairly small business. But what about that moment when someone comes up to you and says: "Would you do a talk on this?", "Would you be happy to come and share with our guys how it works?". "Can you present this to our board?"

What happens? Do you jump at the opportunity? Do you go into hiding? If you say "yes", what happens inside of you? Are you a nervous wreck? Or do you feel strong and have a sense of real excitement?

Imagine you're standing by the coffee machine at your co-working space, when the CEO stands next to you looking worried. "What's wrong?" you ask.

"We've been asked to give a talk."

"That's great!"

The CEO says "We've built a great business, great cash flow and have an awesome product, but we aren't public speakers... Jon won't do it, Rosie gets too nervous, Bob is too wild, Salim lacks stage presence and Ron will talk about himself the whole time. It's such a great opportunity but I think we'll have to turn it down."

He continues, "I could do it, but I wouldn't be any good. I'd end up doing more harm than good. I'd love the exposure, but it's not going to happen."

There are three outcomes to this situation:

1. Pass it over and do nothing.
2. Get some training quickly.
3. Ask a gifted public speaker to represent you.

Which would you choose?

It's a real-life example, and the CEO chose the third option, asking Annik, my co-founding partner of Speaker Express, to represent the company. This scenario is surprisingly common. Most people will either say "no" or they do it and don't do a great job, so business opportunities are lost.

There are all kinds of other scenarios where you could feel stuck:

- Maybe you are used to pitching in front of friendly angel investors and now have to pitch to a room full of serious venture capitalists.
- You are being asked to convince the board of directors about a new project.
- You are asked to share your expert knowledge on an industry panel discussion.
- You are invited to speak in front of your industry peers at a breakfast networking morning.
- You are asked to speak and present an industry award.
- You have been invited to present a keynote speech at an industry conference.
- You have an opportunity to pitch your product at an industry competition.
- You receive your first ever invitation to represent your company in a prestigious forum.

People use public speaking for so many different reasons. Here are a few examples of people who came to Speaker Express looking for help:

- A CEO who had single-handedly built his business to a team of 20 people wanted to hold inspiring team meetings and be respected. At the time, he struggled with motivating his team because nerves got the better of him.
- A former Goldman Sachs account manager, turned tech entrepreneur, wanted to learn how to tell his brand story and pitch better.
- A Managing Director of a marketing company wanted to learn to sell better from stage.
- The Managing Director of a loan business wanted to scale up, but knew he had to go from one-on-one meetings to group presentations to sell his products and services.
- A food tech entrepreneur wanted to make the jump from chef to international consultant.

All of those people trained with Speaker Express and these are the results:

- The CEO no longer suffers from imposter syndrome and can hold effective inspirational team talks.
- The tech entrepreneur has now raised over a million pounds in funding.
- The MD of the marketing company now gets a continuous flow of leads when he speaks.
- The MD of the loan business has since expanded his business to three other cities in the UK.
- The food tech entrepreneur gained confidence and understanding of how to build a speaking business. This enabled her to speak internationally and get paid for the privilege.

The aim of this book is to help you add public speaking to your toolkit so that you can accelerate the growth of your business. If you want to build a speaking business, this book can get you started with that too. Speaking can magnify your positioning as the Founder, CEO, Entrepreneur or Managing Director, as well as support you in getting you and your brand more visibility. This, in turn, will create more leads and generate more sales. This is what lies at the heart of Speaker Express and is how we've been getting great results for clients just like you since 2011.

The next time you're asked to do a talk, we want you to be able to jump at the opportunity, knowing that your speaking will inspire and motivate the audience and, of course, convert into business opportunities.

If you're feeling doubtful, let me illustrate the transformation that's possible by telling you Annik's story.

In 2009, in order to graduate, Annik had to participate in a group presentation. She had six weeks' notice, and she spent every one of those 42 days listening to the negative voices in her head, and convincing herself how awful her time on stage would be. When the day came, it was awful. Annik had sweaty palms, shaking knees, a pounding heart in a burning body, but she also had something else: the determination to face her anxieties and never feel like this again.

Two years later, Annik and I ran the first ever Speaker Express Club Night in a dingy pub basement in Islington with 20 people. By confronting her fears and being gentle with herself while she learned, Annik finally had her breakthrough – after 30 years of being scared of public speaking.

Who Is Writing This Book?

From Dancer to International Speaker

Now that I've told you Annik's story, I'll tell you briefly about my own beginnings and what's led me to a career in, and passion for, public speaker training.

I started out my professional career as a dancer, yep a fully-fledged dancer who toured the world doing various forms of contemporary dance. I started dancing very late, at the age of 21, and had to work my little behind off to make a career of it. I was absolutely loving the dance touring lifestyle until suddenly I suffered a back injury, and just like that my dream came crumbling down and I had to stop dancing.

This of course caused me to re-evaluate where to go next in life. Have you ever hit a crossroads? One that gets you to re-examine everything you have worked so hard for and now it all appears to be gone?

Whilst they both involve a stage, presence and engaging with an audience, expressing yourself as a dancer is very different to moving a crowd through speaking. Speaking was not on my radar initially, and I ended up speaking very much by accident in a roundabout way...

When my career as a dancer ended, my life became much more conventional. Initially, I secured a job, found a nice house and lived the corporate worker lifestyle. Because I was a hard worker, I rose very quickly to be a trainer for some of the UK's leading blue-chip brands.

Yet in my soul, there was a hole. There was a gap in my life that nothing seemed to fill. Know that feeling? Well, that's what I was carrying around. It turned out to be the entrepreneur in me. Even whilst working full time, I always had a side hustle, such as producing a pilot for TV which got very close to being accepted, working as PR for a modelling agency and attempting to launch a fashion label. I got so far in my side ventures, but never far enough.

Once I got promoted to training roles, I started to find my flow again and really fell in love with it. The real breakthrough in terms of speaking came when I realised I had gone as far as I could as a trainer without a training qualification. I started to seek ways to progress my career and looked at qualifications. I spent hours googling and reading about which qualification was the best, eventually landing on a coaching certification which I knew would help me become a better trainer.

This was an old-school training course which meant I had to work with 15 case studies and do many tests. As part of the training, I took it upon myself to go and watch other coaches speak. It was at a big self-development seminar that I had my moment of realisation.

This man I had never heard of walked onto the stage, and owned it. He was so powerful, moving and engaging. I'd originally intended to only stay for one day. However, I ended staying for the whole three days. I felt this childlike excitement. I watched this guy like a kid watching their favourite movie. I was hooked. I watched the incredible power of this guy standing on stage and the way he could move people. It was amazing.

"Why can't I do that?" I thought. It had nothing to do with the money-making aspect; it had more to do with the impact. Witnessing the effect that one person could have on a room of 5,000 people for three days blew me away. I had found my new form of dance, metaphorically speaking. I thought, given that I 'd already done over 1,000 hours of dance performance, it would be an easy transition. But I was very wrong.

A lot of people who used to be performers make that same mistake. After doing a couple of speaking gigs, I learnt the hard way that I would need to retrain and almost start all over again; I was used to using my body, but not my mouth. I enrolled in public speaking training, took weeks out to attend these trainings and still do. It's like anything: you have to keep training to keep your standards high. I would immerse myself in the intensive trainings which were often 18-hour days for 12 days at a time.

Then, between training sessions, I spent thousands of hours training by myself to a high standard. I used to take a whole week off before my seminars to practise, drill the detail, and work on all aspects of speaking delivery. This is how my seminar Power to Succeed grew so quickly and went from 58 in the room to 150-200 every other month for three years, enabling me to build my coaching at that time into a six-figure business.

I no longer run Power To Succeed, but since then I have delivered hundreds of different talks in the UK, the US, Africa and the Middle East – and the list keeps on growing. Of course, I also deliver most of the trainings for Speaker Express, and have helped to build the training as well as the business as a whole.

> *We are a big advocate of the concept #useyourvoiceforgood.*
>
> *Your words have the power to change the world, as long as you use them in an ethical way. Just stop and reflect on that power you could have, and how you would want to use it.*

How To Get The Most From This Book

Before we get going with this book, I want you to take some time to consider and answer these questions:

- What is it that you want from public speaking?
- How can you see public speaking growing your business?
- What are your personal motivations?

Take some time out to reflect and answer these questions as they will help shape your experience and reasons for reading this book.

When we ask these questions in training sessions, these are some of the most common answers we get:

- Overcoming nerves and confidence issues.
- Learning how to sell better and promote a product/service.
- Getting paid for speaking gigs.
- To be seen as a thought leader.
- Being asked to speak, but feeling you don't have what it takes.
- Getting your brand message out there.
- Signing up more clients and making sales.
- Using speaking as an additional income stream.
- Being seen as an influencer.
- Learning how to pitch better.
- Utilising PR and TV opportunities.

Take time after each chapter to write your own thoughts and takeaways, discuss with a business colleague, or share on social media to affirm what you've learned using @speakerexpress

PART ONE:
Speaking in Business

CHAPTER 1

How Speaking Can Change Hearts and Minds

A good place to start is to explore just how we can be using our voice and the platforms we have to create a better world. Many of the big brands and corporates understand this, although they don't always implement it in a positive way. Think of all the different ways a voice can be used:

- The voice of an individual.
- The voice of a brand or company.
- The voice of an industry.
- The voice of a nation.
- The voice of a community or collective.
- The voice of a cause.

A voice can be used to create a kinder, safer world if you choose to do it. Giving your brand and company a voice and a cause can make local and global impact. While you will use public speaking to grow your business, it can also be used to give a voice to the voiceless, and speak up about what matters. It can be used for so many great reasons, which in turn will change hearts and minds.

Stepping out on stage to use your voice for good is one of the most powerful and important strategies you can implement to grow your business. One of the most impactful ways to reach your customers, your audience and your fans, is by speaking and standing for something; a cause or a movement. By doing this, you connect to the heart of your clients. When you speak for good it is good for business.

We live in an age of authenticity and people want to get to know the who's and whys behind a company. We live in an age when people interview companies for jobs not the other way round.

These days, you can access wisdom within seconds and why wouldn't you want your wisdom to be part of the collective thought leaders out there? From Malala to Branson, why wouldn't you want your wisdom to be among these names? You already use your voice for so many different reasons, right? To warn a child of danger, to share your opinion on politics or the current world events. Why not take that same voice and use it not only to grow your business but to do some good in this world?

We need great leaders and your voice matters.

I haven't always been great at what I do. It is only from delivering 7,000 hours of talks and working as an assistant trainer for 5 years for an international public speaking training company that got me started on this journey. I have, however, always known that I have a voice that can impact people, and if I'm in a position of influence I can use it for good. I aim to inspire as many people as possible to use their voice too, especially entrepreneurs like you.

Recently I went to see a business owner speak. He's one of the most successful people who pitched on Dragons' Den and his story is incredible. I already knew about his success and story, which is inspiring enough, yet when I saw him speak, it was a game changer. He was funny, warm, powerful, vulnerable, insightful and approachable. Now, I see his products very differently. Seeing him changed my relationship with the brand.

> *When your customer gets to hear you, see you, laugh with you, shake your hand, take a selfie with you and bond with you, it changes everything. It changes how they feel about your brand, how they speak about you and how they want to interact with your company.*

There is something rather vibrant and powerful about having an inner driver and the absolute inner determination to get somewhere big. Many admired people – such as Elon Musk, Bill Gates, Steve Jobs, Arianna Huffington – had one important thing to drive them. They each had a vision of a better future for humanity, even without any evidence of their dream ever coming to life. They have all used their voice for good, and in doing so have made a significant impact in their industries as result.

No one we have worked with or listed above got to massive success without using their voice for good, without public speaking and pitching to win over clients. People who understand this and have this attitude fly a lot faster. Get your speaking and your message aligned with your strategy to watch the fireworks go off. It isn't always easy but it is always worth it. Always start before you are ready. So if you are ready or even if you're not – let's do it!

CHAPTER 2

The Public Speaking Industry

The world has changed a lot over the last 10 years, impacting the way industries operate, and has changed again since COVID-19. Technology has evolved, customer demand has sped up and the world of business changes daily. The speaking industry is no exception. When people turn to us and ask about paid speaking gigs, we explain that they aren't around like they used to be and are harder to come by.

What happened? You might remember 2008-9? We had a recession which had a massive knock-on effect on the speaking industry. Then there was COVID-19, changing and disrupting every business and industry once again. Many conferences and speaker-led events tanked and the industry stalled like a lot of the economy. Training and L&D (Learning and Development) budgets were slashed.

Back in 2008-9, I was a trainer at the time for some major blue-chip clients and saw this first-hand. Meetings were put on hold or made virtual, and inspirational/motivational speakers saw a huge chunk of their business vanish overnight. Some speakers lost it all. Then, it happened again in 2020 when COVID-19 hit, and there simply wasn't demand for speaking as we knew it any more from corporate clients. With the economy on life support, companies could hardly justify junkets to exotic locales, even if the benefits were worth it. Most companies were gasping for breath and heading to the unknown. Demand for speakers seemed to come to a halt and the industry has remained careful ever since.

Gradually, after 2008-9 as the economy recovered, the speaking industry started coming back and there still plenty of companies that are happy to pay good money for speakers.

People and businesses started to breathe again. What has been noticeable for me, as someone who uses speaking consistently to grow my business, is the fundamental shift in what is needed from speakers. There's a great emphasis on the content delivered and the value that will be taken away. Everyone who's speaking to grow their business or is a thought leader is now asked to deliver clear 'take-aways' and bookers want to know what these will be and that they will be aligned with their intended outcomes. These take-aways need to be immediate, practical, measurable and crafted with the audience in mind. Businesses and audiences now want more authenticity from speakers, as well as connection and access.

In the past, you could command a fee of a few thousand just because you spoke on a certain topic, with only a handful of others and had the relevant experience. It was a given that you would be paid for your time, have expenses paid and be treated like royalty. Times have changed.

For the minority of high-end speakers that is still the case; think Oprah, Simon Sinek, Deborah Meaden and Sheryl Sandberg. These are people who have made a big dent in their industry and are now household names. However, a lot of profile-building groundwork must be done to reach that point. Perhaps that isn't your ambition and you simply want to speak to grow your business, be seen as an industry expert and win more customers. Either of these approaches works, there is no right or wrong here, just knowing the level *you* want to speak at is enough, which is why having a strong, powerful vision for yourself, your speaking and the company is a must.

Since the shift in the industry, you must now consider so much more than simply being a charismatic speaker with the relevant experience and title. What audiences want right now is a deep, powerful story that will help them make sense of the chaos they're experiencing as consumers. Telling your audience a real story connects your audience to you as well as further enhances your thought leadership and authority. Add in your true character, conflict and personal challenge to the story and we call this an emotional drop. Once dropping your audience into some pain you have experienced, you can tell them what you have learnt from that change and how it applies to them. When you do craft a genuine emotional story, the effect on the audience is magical. They stay engaged for long periods of time.

When speaking these days, you are competing against this amazing thing called a mobile phone which means you can easily have a highly-distracted audience. To rise above the rest, you need to enrol the audience to buy into you, keep their attention and deliver world-class content.

Your job is to rise above the noise, to be seen, be heard and make a dent in your industry while still being authentic.

The days of speaking only being for people who do it naturally or are 'well known' are over. Speaking is no longer for the chosen few. Anyone can learn to speak well, and if you have a business to grow it's an essential part of standing out from your competition. You can do it on a big or small scale, online, offline, locally, globally, internally and/or externally. The doors are wide open for everyone, and social media gives an avenue and platform to reach an audience online.

Being the world's greatest speaker without a stage is like being the world's best Formula 1 driver without a car. People have to know about you to want to see you speak, so for this reason you must think about your written content as much as your spoken word. You must think about your social media presence, how to build followers or, more importantly, a loyal audience. Then, how you convert your audience into paying clients and raving fans. Your talks must be a powerful extension of the rest of your brand. It's no longer enough for speaking to stand alone.

Stop for a second and think. Who are the speakers you have seen who inspire you? What is it about them that gets you all fired up inside?

Integrating speaking as a growth strategy is a very exciting and powerful path to take. The door is truly open.

CHAPTER 3

From Communicator to Influencer

We are living in one of the most exciting times in the history of mankind. Why? Because we have so many different platforms and ways in which we can communicate. With a click, you can have an instant global market. You can have a captive audience of thousands from your bedroom. Your videos can reach millions. You can turn your life into a 24-hour story if you wish. You can talk in photos, videos and send voice messages. You can run courses and talks on WhatsApp. That's just online. There is offline too, the old-school way.

One thing is for sure, you are always communicating. Therefore being a communicator is easy. However, to use communication to influence is hard. To do it with grace, class and style is even harder. Here are the levels from communicator to authority:

Communicator – we all start here and we all do this daily. Some of us do it well; some of us less so.

Speaker – the moment you step on stage or in front of people, you are a speaker. That doesn't mean you're any good at it, but you're taking the next step.

Leader – this is where you stand for something and are open to sharing from the stage. You could be disruptive, or controversial, or inspirational if you want to change something.

Expert – not only are you standing on stage, but you have niched yourself, mastered a certain topic and are a voice for it. You have published collateral: books, blogs, podcasts even, a fairly large online presence, and you're able to pull in a captive audience.

Influencer - through the years, all leaders good or bad, have understood that it isn't about communication; it's about *influence*.

Authority – an authority is a person who is an acknowledged expert, and has also achieved something ground-breaking, or has noticeably and/or globally affected an industry. An authority might have had a Number One *New York Times* best seller. They have also been in their field for many years and are seen to as a go-to authority in their field.

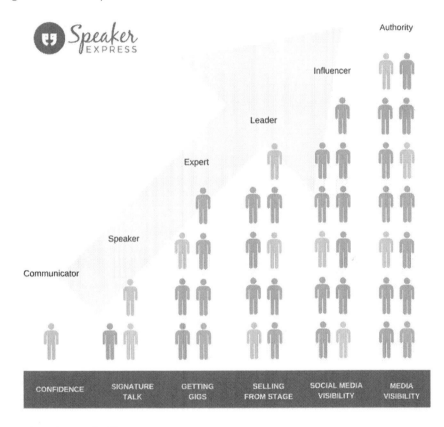

What is an influencer?

- An influencer is an individual who has the power to affect people's decisions, in what they buy or how they vote, because of their authority, knowledge, position or relationship with their audience.

Or, another explanation of an influencer is:

- *An individual who is, or claims to be, an expert with a following in a particular niche. They actively engage with their followers who regard them as the go-to person. The size of their following depends on the size of the niche.*

According to the Q4 Global Digital Statshot report in 2018, 44% of the population are active social media users, which has given birth to a different type of influencer. These are people who have built their following because of their knowledge and/or expertise in a certain area. They post about that topic consistently on their preferred social media channels, and generate large followings of enthusiastic, engaged people. One of the key words is *engaged*. Engagement is sometimes more important than the size (although, in this case, size does matter too).

Typically, there are four types of influencers:

Celebrities – these are the original influencers. Throughout time, they've played a key role in selling the dream, especially if they appear to be living it. (The Kardashians are a modern-day example of this).

Authority/Thought Leaders – they have done the hard work, put in the time and effort to stand out, have published a wealth of information about their topic and have a large following because of this. (Gary Vee, Simon Sinek or Brené Brown are examples).

Bloggers – these are people with a huge online following because of the content they have created, and/or because of their opinion or approach to different aspects of life. Food bloggers are a great example of this. Bloggers have been featured in films, and TV series. They are often invited to write in national papers on their chosen topic. (Kottke is a great example of this; see Kottke.org).

Micro influencers – these are people who dominate a micro niche: a thin but deep market or audience. Normally, they have a following of up to 100,000 and are associated with good causes such as social injustice, environmental issues, or health and wellness. (Daniel Priestley, Founder of Dent and creator of Key Person of Influence, is an example of this).

Our aim is to get you to be seen as an influencer because this is where you can:

- make the most significant impact.
- take your business and brand to a whole new level.
- access more of the financial rewards.
- get other brands and people lining up to put you in front of their staff and ask to consult and hear what you have to say.
- put people in touch with each other who otherwise wouldn't normally connect.
- be introduced to other influencers.

It is truly a wonderful place to be. Public speaking is a great way to not only get there, but also to position yourself as an influencer. How do you do it? By having something interesting to say, saying it in an interesting way and being consistent about saying it. You should say it in many different ways on many different platforms, and today, there are plenty of options.

The harsh reality is that it isn't enough any more to simply be a good communicator. Anyone can be a good communicator, just like anyone can make vanilla ice cream. The truth is that where the influencer goes, the money flows. I will make a wild guess here and trust that the reason you do what you do and are reading this book is because you want to be a force for good in the world and/or in your industry. The best way to do that is go to the top of the tree and influence from there.

Audience psychology

Part of influencing an audience is understanding their psychology. Many speakers deliver really great talks, but when it comes to selling and/or promoting, they change, and their energy is different. They can become tense or apologetic because they're not comfortable with selling. You have to remember that from the moment you are standing on stage, you are selling – selling yourself, selling the brand and/or the company. Whatever issues you have around sales, you need to get over them – fast.

It helps to realise that there are different types of people in the audience. Please understand this isn't about putting people in boxes, it is about being aware of how people will show up when you speak and how you can deal with them.

Before I go into these different types of audience members, I want to first introduce some rules of thumb of how **you** can react and respond to your audience. Encompassing these will help to keep you grounded and strong no matter who's in the crowd:

- **Don't take it personally** – when people attend talks, they have their own stuff going on in their head, and will have their own opinions. Let them say what they need to say, acknowledge them for expressing their thoughts, and either offer to speak to them later or simply move on, letting them know that they are entitled to their opinion.

- **Detach and let go** – if they persist, don't argue or let them goad you into debate. Remember that there are other people in the audience. If they see one person do it, they will also start to do it, and you will lose them. Ask them more questions, get more understanding of their starting point, and either address their concerns there and then, or offer to address them offline because you have to continue with your talk. You must respect everyone's time.

- **Use humour where it works**: a lot of public speakers talk about using humour to defuse these situations. This can certainly help; however this is where your experience counts. Done properly, it works. Done badly, you lose the audience. Experience and being funny will help you.

Different types of people who attend talks:

The Raving Fan – they hang on to every word you say, they love you and always want to come to make themselves known to you, and give you their support. They are likely to want to work with you, and will tell loads of people about you and your company.

The Learner – they are there to learn about your content. They are likely to have already checked you out online. They will want to hear more and could become clients with the right content.

The Authority – normally, they are an authority. Make sure when they speak that you recognise them and give them respect, even if they disagree with you. There is a reason they are there, so find out what it is and have a respectful discussion. If needs be, involve the audience to get a range of opinions. Then check that you have addressed their concerns or comments and move on.

The "Yeah But" Person – they insist on asking lots of questions and whatever your answer, they always seem to use the line "yeah, but". Give them some attention to address their "yeah, but", and if this doesn't work, use fact and proof and make sure you keep the audience onside. If they continue, either ask them to be quiet, if they mind if you move on, or leave, but always do this with respect.

The Sceptic – they will question you and look to catch you out. When they find that you are who you say you are and prove that you do deliver what you say you will, they will quickly become your greatest fan. Welcome their questions and their awkwardness, as when you win them over, the audience will love you that much quicker. Learn to love the sceptic.

The Jibber Jabber – this is the person who babbles a lot without any real point. Hear them out and then ask them to sum up what they have to say in three sentences and then carry on.

The Dominator – the one who wants to hog the mic' and take over; the one who feels they should be up there speaking and thinks they are an "authority" even when they are not. When you have one, very quickly let them have their say, thank them for it and then move to the next person. If they keep going, call them out on it and remind them there are other members of the audience who you also want to address. They might say things like, "I think you are wrong", "Have you thought that you need to do it this way...?", "After my experience in...", "You should listen to what I have to say." You must be in your certainty when dealing with dominators.

CHAPTER 4

Speaking Accelerates Growth

We have seen founders of tech start-ups go from being nervous wrecks to winning speaking awards, being invited on to panels and becoming paid keynote speakers. This has led to more exposure for their start-up, database growth, more clients and accelerated profits. Many coaches become sought after and have people lining up to work with them as a result of giving a powerful talk.

Pitch yourself as an expert

It is a simple fact that once you stand on stage, something happens in the mind of the person watching you. You are often instantly elevated to expert status: people listen and take on board what you have to say. Someone once said: "If you want to be perceived as the expert, swap place from being IN the audience to being ON stage." Your first talk might not be as good as your eighth but start somewhere, get trained. Put in the hours and get yourself out there.

Accelerate sales

Instead of closing one sale per day, you'll be able to close numerous in one go, bringing in up to 6 figures worth of business. Instead of doing 10 one-on-one conversations per week, you can generate the same outcome from just one speaking gig to 80 people and convert them after you finish your 45-minute talk at a conference.

Even if your aim isn't to be a speaker, having speaking as a tool will accelerate the growth of your business.

As an entrepreneur, you have put in a lot of hard work building a business – but then you need to speak about what you have done, pitch it, promote and enrol people into your vision.

Why now?

- It could be because you have invested in a new online platform; or maybe you've built one and it needs users.
- Maybe your service or product service is bloody good, but not enough people are hearing about it.
- You have a huge vision and want to reach like-minded people.
- You just want to communicate better with your staff.
- Maybe you want more people to hear your brand story.
- You want to feel free and in control for 'ad hoc' speaking opportunities.
- You might be wondering about the best way to lead your existing presentation to more sales in line with your brand values.

Speaker training can also help you in other and unexpected areas of your business. A consultant recently came to us who loved our trainings and knew she could benefit from them. She had a very good contract but when it was time to negotiate the new terms she wanted to increase her fees and be paid more. This is where our training came in handy. She credits her ability to get higher rates to the training she received from us. Public speaking also trains you in negotiations and skills for life, which will in turn grow your business.

CHAPTER 5

Speaking as a Tool for Business Impact

Having worked with thousands of business owners and entrepreneurs, I have seen too many underestimate the importance of using public speaking as a business tool. Those who embrace it are rewarded with an increased profile, a bigger reach and the ability to select their opportunities, compared to constantly having to hustle just to be considered.

At Speaker Express, we believe that every entrepreneur should have a voice that leads them to business growth, while doing good in their industry.

We have seen powerful people who are incredible entrepreneurs, pioneers and innovators but who are crippled with fear and overwhelming nerves when it comes to speaking. As a result, people are left scared and not wanting to stand in front of an audience, limiting the influence they can have in their industry. Not hearing these people share their ideas, creations, innovations, content and what they have to offer is a real loss. A loss to themselves, their businesses and industries. How many businesses go under due to lack of sales? Due to lack of visibility? Or because the founders or creators are busy creating and not selling enough?

Be humble: the importance of training to develop speaker skills

Like most things worth doing, public speaking takes time and effort. To truly master the art of public speaking requires constant tweaking and improving. You should train, but also always look to improve your level of delivery, as well as clocking up hours of experience giving talks.

We regularly see entrepreneurs missing out on opportunities, losing out on sales and potential long-term customers. My heart breaks a little every time I hear of a small or big business going down, even though I know they had a great business or team, and they were a great company doing great things for this world. What hurts is knowing how much can be changed and rectified simply with a little bit of training. There are few skills that will bring more opportunity into your business life than the ability to speak well. It will open doors for joint ventures and improve sales.

It isn't just confidence issues that can interfere with your ability to speak. There is the other extreme: speakers thinking that just because they are confident enough they don't need training, structure, understanding of audience psychology or content flow. We once hired a speaker who had an amazing online profile, but his speaking ability really did not match that, his speaking skills were outright awful and reflected badly on us as a speaking training company to have him speaking at our event. We had lots of people come up to us at the end of the night wondering how he got on our stage? Everyone can have a bad day, but what made it worse was he wasn't open to feedback, he didn't want to listen. He was convinced he was brilliant. Do you know someone like that? Situations like this can harm your brand and impact your sales equally.

The irony is that a lot of successful people out there are the ones who are the least complacent and most dedicated to personal improvement and training. Successful people I've met seem to be the most open-minded to growth, training and to be working on the little as well as the big things. As I am writing this book, we just finished interviewing a whole bunch of businesses that turned over £2 million last year and one thing they have in common is never-ending improvement for their companies and themselves as people.

Stand for something

Speaker Express's mission is to help as many businesses as possible to create meaningful content that will help them grow. This is our big 'why'. We care about your journey and your ability to make an impact in the world. For us, knowing that people engage with their speaking ability is exciting. We would love to hear your big why too. Message us on Instagram or the Speaker Express page on Facebook @speakerexpress.

Connecting with your core message, what you stand for and sharing it on stage can also have side effects while having an amazing impact on your business.

For example: a digital business consultant who came to us for advice was initially convinced that her big message was business related. She enrolled to work with us and showed up on her first day ready for training. Her intention was to nail her business message and be able to communicate it. As the day unfolded, she watched speaker after speaker (all business owners and entrepreneurs) in the training room sharing their messages with strong impact, yet powerful vulnerability. Something inside her changed and the training awoke something that she didn't see coming.

The next morning, she stood up and shared her personal story. Everyone went silent, gripped by it and what she'd had to cope with. While her story wasn't related to her business, the impact of her standing up and speaking authentically and vulnerably had a life-changing effect on her and her mission. She realised the power of standing on stage, there and then, and how this could help her cause. As a result of the experience, she then went on to launch a campaign to tackle and change the law around rape in the UK (needless to say, not an easy mission). Within two weeks, she had raised £20,000 to fight her legal case; she ended up appearing on multiple TV interviews, and raising her issue in Parliament, supported by five parties. Two years later, she is still regularly asked to appear as an expert on a variety of issues related to women on BBC radio stations and Sky News.

She didn't enrol to work with us with that intention, however, that is where she ended up and her life has changed since. Now she also charges £6,000 to deliver digital workshops, which was her original reason for joining. When you allow a journey to unfold, you end up in unexpected places – just like the wonderful Emily Hunt who I have spoken about here.

Decide your next steps

Would you like more influence in your industry or market? Would you like to create more impact? Would you like to add a few zeros to your turnover? Speaking is a powerful addition to any solid business strategy, that can help you towards any of those goals, and the next few chapters contain the secrets to unlocking the next level of speaking for you.

Your next steps might jump right out at you or you might need to read through a few chapters for enhanced clarity. It is essential that you read each page rather than simply focusing in on the one aspect you think you need the most, as they all work in unison. I will give you clear instructions on to how to apply the lessons you get from reading this book as we go along.

My aim by the end of the book is to have shown you how you can use public speaking to enhance the potential of your business. It won't happen simply by sitting on the couch reading, of course, just like thinking about running a marathon won't prepare you for those 26.2 miles. But what I can do is cover the core methodology and prepare you before you start putting what you learn here into practice.

Introducing: The Speakers' Method

Now for the fun part, the 6 core areas as part of The Speakers' Method that can help you get there. This is a methodology that has matured since 2011, seeing results of thousands of people coming through our trainings.

The 6 core areas include:

- **Confidence**

  No matter the level you are as a speaker, there is always room for improvement. The first step is to work on your confidence, taking you from beginner to experienced, from meeting rooms to large audiences. Confidence sits at the heart of speaking and it is the key to unlocking more sales and business success.

- **Brand Message**

  Your brand's tone of voice is incredibly important. How do you want your business to be seen, heard and felt? Brand Message creation will make sure that what you say lands correctly with your ideal customers and creates brand loyalty, leading to a tribe that returns to buy from you again and again.

- **Signature Talk**

  Your Signature Talk will be a proven structure that you can deliver time and time again, with consistent results. It will routinely bring in leads, sales and make an impact every time you deliver it. This structure helps you without coming across as being pushy.

- **Getting Booked**

  This is about understanding industry secrets and what event organisers, bureaus and agents are looking for, as well as the differences between the 3. We also cover different ways you can get repeat bookings appropriate for your business, brand and industry. Following a proven process and understanding the main requirements of paid speaking gigs will also increase your chances of being approached and selected.

- **Pitch & Sales**

  The best speakers turn their talks into cash, and it's something you can do to leverage more sales and recognition. We will teach you how to use speaking to sell your brand, products and services in a way that is in line with your brand values and who you are as a business.

- **Building Your Profile**

  Every time you speak, capturing photos, video recordings, testimonials or endorsements will help develop your profile, and increase your online and offline visibility. This will generate repeat bookings and new opportunities and get you onto bigger stages. Every time this happens the profile and visibility of your business and brand will grow.

Including these in your business toolbox will help you to:

- Improve your ability to sell your ideas.
- Have a wider range to express yourself – online and offline.
- Reach a wider audience quicker.
- Become a better negotiator.
- Increase your ability to inspire and motivate your team.
- Raise your expert status.
- Help you to connect with your community/tribe at a deeper level.
- Make more money.

Arrive: have your "moment"

You might do some short and some long presentations. For example, I currently deliver anything from ten minutes to two days. As you deliver more and more talks, you will reach a point when you have your "**moment**". Every speaker has the moment when they have **arrived**. Boom!

The moment when you have fully taken control of your speaking looks something like this:

- Your opening has impact.
- The stories you tell have their desired effect and at the end people line up to speak to you.
- You feel powerful and in your flow.
- People are waiting for you afterwards to talk business.

That's the "moment". Everything lands, and then you will truly understand the power and impact of public speaking. Most of the time, people are aware of this. But when they *experience* it, it is powerful and even life-changing. We have seen this over and over again when running trainings, whether it be our two-day Creating your Signature Talk event or our Speaking Accelerator programmes. Clients often send us emails or tag us in a social media post to thank us, sharing their "moment" when everything clicked into place. It moves us every time. It truly changes people's lives. That is the power of public speaking and with it comes the realisation that it can have the most profound impact on growing your business.

PART TWO:
Deep Dive into
The Speakers' Method

During this second part, we will delve into six core elements that make your impact more powerful, both as a business and speaker.

This is an effective, yet simple, system to help you build a business that uses speaking as a growth strategy. All our trainings and teaching stem from this methodology, which has been devised and honed over the last 8 years.

I hope by now it has become clear why speaking must be an essential part of your strategy. From here on, we will break down the Speakers' Method and how you can apply these teachings in practice. The following chapters have taken thousands of hours from our training sessions and translated them into simple concepts and steps, whilst weaving in some helpful stories and case studies.

CHAPTER 6

The Speakers' Method: Confidence

The ability to deliver your talk with clarity, confidence and impact: free flowing and natural, in control of your words, thoughts and physiology. This is usually the first goal for anyone new to public speaking.

Just to be clear, confidence is not about being loud and shouty. Just think of Oprah, who has grace and a thoughtful and connected delivery style. Confidence is the ability to project that you know what you are talking about 100%, as well as being able to remain calm under pressure and keep going when things don't go as planned.

As speakers, we can get frustrated with feeling nervous; we want to overcome this and the nerves to go. But nerves are common, felt by almost everyone when speaking, and they stick despite your level of experience. Nerves are the biggest deterrent to speaking. So why is it that we are so terrified of public speaking?

The Neuroscience of nerves and negative thoughts

The racing heart, the shaky legs, the sweaty palms. We want them gone. Then we can get on with the important business of communicating our message.

Growing up, many of us didn't learn how to fully process emotions. We bottle them up or count to ten and wait for the 'nerve storm' to subside. However, emotions are messages; thoughts delivered from the brain into the body. We can't simply turn that pathway off. We are hardwired to *feel*.

When we lived in the wild, with sabre-toothed tigers over the hill looking for dinner, we relied on those feelings. Something as small as an unfamiliar scent could trigger a surge of fear that would propel us into action and an injection of adrenaline to help us sprint away from possible death. You'll know this as the 'fight or flight' response. Although we've evolved in many ways, this primal response is still very much present.

When we take to the stage to speak, it can feel, quite literally, like life or death. Potential physical threats have been replaced by imagined social threats.

If you truly want to have massive impact on stage, you cannot outwit, reject or deny your feelings. They demand one simple thing: to be accepted, to be felt. The lifetime of an emotion, if felt, is said to be about 90 seconds. Conversely, if bottled up or pushed down, it will linger, grow stronger, and ultimately become paralysing.

This acceptance is not mental or theoretical, it's a practical skill, executed – just as emotions are – through the body. The butterflies, the sweating, the pounding head, twisted guts and beating heart – these fear-related discomforts must be accepted, welcomed, felt. Then, like a sparkler, they quickly burn themselves out.

Simple, but not easy. And only then, when we've 'felt first', can we begin the business of thinking.

Another thing to understand before we can know how to deal with nerves is the science of negative thinking. We have thousands of thoughts – many of them not even conscious. Judging by the state of humanity and the number of people scared of public speaking or worried about what others think about them, many of these thoughts are negative.

As soon as we are consciously thinking a negative thought such as 'Oh my god, there are 400 people out there in the audience, I haven't prepared enough, who am I to talk about the future of food technology...' many of us can continue this negative downward thought spiral. Negative thoughts cause our bodies to release chemical responses such as cortisol and adrenaline, leading to the fight-or-flight response. Always remember in that situation there is no physical threat to run away from although it feels that way.

When we are on stage, all too often we block the creative side of our brain when trying to remember our material and get into a state of overthinking instead of being present, which is essential. Being present is where audience connection and rapport is at its best. Not believing the thoughts or giving them too much attention, but simply observing and allowing them to pass, helps you to stay present in the moment.

Dealing with nerves

If you're thinking about waiting until you're more confident to begin speaking from stage, think again. It comes with experience. Don't wait. Start before you think you are ready and present, despite the doubts and fears. Get started at a small storytelling platform or give a speech over Christmas dinner.

Nerves become heightened from the fear of things going wrong. Funnily enough, the reality is that often when speaking, things will go wrong. You will say something and then think, 'that really sounded better in my head', or you will forget to say something you intended to include. When these things happen it's always OK, and never as problematic as to warrant the level of nerves and worry we have. The nerves that come up before a talk usually stem from 'what if' thoughts, such as:

- What if I forget my structure for what to say or go blank?
- What if I forget some of the content?
- What if people find me boring or uninteresting?
- What if someone walks out of the room?
- What if things go wrong that make me look unprofessional?

- What if someone makes a derogative comment or contradicts me?

All the above trigger different internal reactions:

- The voice in your head spirals negatively.
- Your heartbeat speeds up, as does your breathing.
- Your mind suddenly goes blank and you lose your flow.

These reactions can feel quite daunting and put people off speaking completely, but they can be dealt with easily in the moment and quickly overcome. Let's tackle these scenarios one by one:

The voice in your head spirals negatively: If the voices in your head are going off, accept them and consciously tell yourself, 'It's okay! This is normal'. This will be much more beneficial than questioning 'Why am I feeling this way?'. Also, don't be afraid to tell your voices to be quiet (in your head!) and balance out the negative voices by consciously adding some positive reinforcement such as "I am a confident person and I know my stuff". Having your own mantra you can really help with this.

Your heartbeat speeds up, as does your breathing: This will often result in you talking very quickly and rushing through your presentation. The best way to reverse this is to slow down your breathing. Pause and take a deep breath, then say one sentence veeery slowly with lots of pausing to completely alter your pace and back down. Once you slow your breathing and get more oxygen into your lungs, your heart will calm down.

Your mind suddenly goes blank and you lose your flow: One of the first things to remember is that no one besides you knows your talk. Even if you get something wrong, no one else will know. It's important to very quickly accept that you went wrong, take a deep breath, and keep going even it's to a different point in your talk. Once you get talking again you will re-find your flow and you can always circle back to a missed point if necessary. One great way to win some thinking time is to say something like: 'I want you to really think about what I just said. How can you apply this to your business?' Firstly, this will give you time to breathe and calmly remember what's next. Secondly, it will give the audience time to absorb the information up until that point. Remember, pauses are your friend.

The more you speak and gain experience, the more you will find different ways to deal with these situations and the nerves will fade. Once you have had to face a situation, it loses its' 'scariness' and, slowly but surely, your comfort zone broadens. When you realise that 'failing' doesn't make you a 'failure', you automatically give yourself permission to try new things outside of your comfort zone, inevitability leading to more growth.

Find your own nerve-tackling strategy

Create your own toolkit for dealing with nerves by finding what works best for you. Eventually you want to have built a little routine that you do every time before giving a talk that builds your confidence and helps you prepare. This could be made up of:

- Breathing techniques.
- Meditations.
- Exercise.
- Emotional Freedom Technique (Tapping).
- Visualisation.
- Neuro-Linguistic Programming.
- Havening.
- Hypnotherapy.
- Reframing.
- Affirmation.
- Praying.

You will find millions of practitioners worldwide on any of the above techniques or you can find out more by diving into YouTube to experiment. You will ideally find a technique that works for you, and integrate it into your life, using it on a regular basis – obviously, in addition to solid planning; prepare your presentation.

We have found these to be some of the most effective ways to deal with nerves:

Breathing – if you feel your breathing gets faster and your heartbeat races, slow down and force yourself to breathe deep breaths; adjust your breathing to a rhythmic flow. Breathing into your diaphragm is required to signal to your body that there is no physical danger to run away from. Avoid the shallow chest breathing.

Mindfulness meditation – if you find yourself in your head, overthinking, slowly look around and find:

- 5 things you can see;
- 4 things you can touch;
- 3 things you can hear;
- 2 things you can smell, or even more powerfully, think of 2 smells you like;
- 1 emotion you feel.

This really helps when you feel like you have gone too far into your head (buying into all those detrimental thoughts) and lost control of your surroundings. This gets you present in the moment.

Grounding – imagine you are firmly connected to the ground, no matter how fast your head keeps spinning with thoughts. You are firmly breathing into your fears, don't force them away, be with them, try to make friends with the often-unpleasant feelings.

Visualisation – visualisation or guided imagery is all about positive thinking, it can be referred to as mental rehearsal too. Many artists, athletes, sportsmen and public figures use this strategy to gain self-confidence and relax before making a speech or giving a talk. Research indicates that positive thinking can improve both physical and mental performance.

There are lots of different things you could visualise, here are my suggestions:

1. Your Introduction
    How well you open your talk, how it goes smoothly and seamlessly. You should start by visualising your introduction. How the audience is looking at you with interest, hanging on your every word, smiling, and the good feelings that come with a great opening.

2. The Audience
    It is important to visualise the audience's reaction, because it's often what people fear the most when they think about giving a talk. How many times do people think about things going wrong vs visualising things going right? *Your speech is all about the audience…not about you. It's about adding value to them and showing you're the expert to solve their problem.* Imagine your audience doing exactly what you want them to do when you're delivering your speech.

3. Body Language
    See the confident version of yourself, standing there with ease. Imagine you are walking confidently around the stage, always an image of calmness.

4. Pausing
    Part of coming across confidently during a talk is having the certainty to ask a question and pause for an answer, or make a statement and pause. Speaking slowly, make sure they are part of the visualisation.

5. The Ending

   Visualise the closing of the talk – how you want it to end and people clapping you or, if you really want to, a standing ovation. If you are selling, visualise people queueing up to buy your product. Always when visualising add the feel-good factor to each part!

Here's what I do to keep my nerves steady before getting on stage.

First, I run before a gig. I also play two or three songs. I mix the songs up: some are more grounding and some are high-energy (8 Mile by Eminem or Edge of Glory by Lady Gaga). I find the mix of high-energy and grounding centres me. I also use what I call a 'Power Call' which is: *"I command my subconscious to allow me to show up in certainty"* and say a prayer: "God allow me to serve this audience to the best of my ability, to empower them and add value to their lives."

Before getting on stage, the co-founder of Speaker Express, Annik, prefers to think of her life as this big canvas and every speaking gig she does is a flick of paint on this masterpiece she is creating. Over the years, the little early 'screw-ups' won't be visible any more. No matter who you are and what you do, there will always be someone who doesn't like you, and that's okay. If you have a message that will solve someone else's problem, then it's your responsibility to get out there and speak up so they can find you.

We have a booklet called 'How To Deal With Nerves' on our website: simply go to https://tinyurl.com/stgnervesbooklet
Password: highgatespeaker

Building confidence

Once the nerves are tackled, you can focus on building up your levels of confidence. There are three levels of confidence that we generally notice develop in our clients through our courses.

Level 1: 'I can do this'

This is when you develop an unshakeable belief in your abilities. You can control your nerves and maintain composure. As a speaker, it means that you can deliver to the best of your ability each and every time. Most people start training with this goal in mind; this is the aim for almost all of our clients. Once you reach this level of confidence it is easy for you to get out on stages speaking. You will then be stretched to move into the next level of confidence.

Level 2: 'I can deliver consistent quality and deal with the unexpected'

Let's paint a picture: you've practised your talk around 50 times; you have perfected the look and design of the slides, helping you remember the structure. You have drilled your closing line and everything is in place for your talk. You arrive at the venue, your heart is pumping with excitement. You see the people coming in; some have travelled a long way to attend. Everyone has taken their seat and the event has begun. You hear the host read out your introduction to start the talk, and you come on stage to a huge round of applause. You grab your clicker, walk to the middle of the stage and start your talk.

However, the mic doesn't work and the big screen suddenly goes blank, not displaying your slides. Even though you know your material, the correct structure is triggered by the sequence of your slides. Everything that you practised goes out of the window.

These types of things can throw even the most accomplished speakers. And there are plenty of other things that can go wrong!

However, it is how you manage this type of situation which shows Level 2 confidence. This is the ability to rescue the situation in a way that empowers you and leaves you shining brightly. The audience is hardly affected, and you still deliver brilliantly. This is Level 2 confidence. It takes time and experience to achieve this.

Here are some other scenarios that could go wrong, which would require you to be at level 2 confidence:

- The train you are on is delayed and you arrive late, unable to set up properly.
- The other speaker doesn't show and you are asked to extend your presentation.
- You or the venue doesn't have the right adapter for your laptop.
- The slides you sent the organiser are suddenly formatted in a different way, looking rather unprofessional.
- You use the wrong version of your slides and there are typos.
- The speaker before you overruns and your timeslot is cut short by the organiser.
- The audience profile is different to what the organiser briefed you on and your examples don't land.
- You expected a quiet room, but it's an area with a lot of noise from speakers in other rooms and exhibition traffic.

Most of these things have happened to me; some have happened to our clients. They are all part of being a professional speaker; the ability to adapt and be agile is hard to teach in the training room and develops through real experience on real stages.

Level 3: 'I am authentic, detached and in flow'

Being calmly confident is the ultimate level of confidence. It's when you are able to simply remain calm regardless of what happens. It is the quiet assurance that means you can see the whole picture, make brilliant decisions from a place of peace, composure and in a relaxed manner. It is a true sign of leadership; you don't need to shout or get sweaty, as you are assured by your certainty and inner belief. It's the ability to command a room from a place of peace, the ability to handle hecklers with a smile on your face and to carry on when everything else appears to be collapsing. To reach this level takes a lot of time, practice and self-work. It is beautiful to witness.

For example, I remember when I used to run Power To Succeed; my two-day seminar. One weekend, after a lot of practising, my moment arrived. I heard my intro, two hundred people in the room. I could feel the energy. The room was vibrant, nervous and explosive. The last sentence of the intro had gone and I walked on stage to a standing ovation. From that moment onwards everything flowed, my stories were bringing people to tears (in a good way). My jokes were landing and I was funny. My content was hitting home and helping people. Everything was flowing in the right way down the river with no effort. My sales pitch was smooth and people got up to join my program. When things went wrong, I took them in my stride and it didn't throw me or take me out of my flow. It was like the whole two days flew by in a blink of an eye – truly beautiful. That's mastery, and what I always aim for.

Confident selling

Another aspect of confidence is the ability to sell your products or services without any guilt, fear or nerves. The more confident you are, the more at ease your audience will feel. The more confidence you have, the better your message is communicated and received and the more you can sell.

Many people have confidence issues when it comes to selling. The biggest fear is that no one will buy. To avoid this, the first step is to know your products and services inside out and have a strong pitch that presents them in a way that your market will relate to. Having a strong pitch you believe in will help you to feel confident in your offering. Keep the offer simple and easy, don't try selling too many things at the same time as a confused mind tends to say 'no'. You can find more detail on this in the 'Pitch and Sales' chapter later on.

Another issue people often have around selling confidently is that they tend to feel guilty selling and/or asking for money for their products and services. These worries often come from past experiences and how they have felt when 'being sold to', and not wanting to appear pushy. But this type of thinking can be very destructive for your revenue flow. Try to reframe the sales in your mind to focus on the value you want to offer to clients and how it could help them, rather than the money you are asking for in exchange.

If you still feel uncomfortable selling, it's important to reflect on this and explore where this feeling is coming from. It could be that you don't think people will pay what you charge, and self-worth issues are getting in the way of your sales results. Or it could be that you simply have deep-rooted challenges with money (you wouldn't be the first person) and this can be for different reasons.

The best thing you can do is deal with any issues you might have around money. There are many different ways of dealing with this, by seeking out a professional therapist. It is ok to make money, it is ok to charge people, and it is ok to sell what you have to offer. Your beliefs are important, and if you don't believe these things in your gut it will effect your sales, so I'd suggest looking for help to change them.

Know that whatever entrepreneurial path you have taken, you have earned the right to sell. Just make sure you do it with grace at the same time as respecting your audience. Do it in the way you would like to be sold to.

Confident body language

Have you ever been told not to use your hands because they distract the audience from what you say? Once, I was told to keep my hands by my side, imagining I am holding 2 sacks of potatoes! This now makes me laugh out loud, simply because it goes so much against my natural flow as a speaker. You can imagine how my ability to engage an audience deteriorated because I was now focused on not using my hands instead of being fully present with my audience and my content.

Our bodies play a role in how we think. When speaking next, just observe what your hands, arms or legs are naturally wanting to do. One could even go as far as saying that your movements double up as a 'second language' to enhance or even add what your words have left out.

In 2015, a study analysing thousands of TED talks (TED is a non-profit devoted to spreading ideas, usually in the form of short, powerful talks – TED stands for Technology, Entertainment and Design) found that the most viewed, viral speakers used an average of 465 hand gestures, nearly twice as many as the less viewed speakers. This research was led by Vanessa Van Edwards – behavioural investigator at her human behaviour research lab, the Science of People.

Intensive studies have been carried out reaching the conclusion that, for example, open palms at a 45-degree angle communicate 'I'm being honest'. Hands hidden send a non-trusting message – apparently, that stems back from when cavemen's hands were the first thing we looked at when seeing a fellow person to check for spears or other weapons.

First and foremost, when starting out as a speaker your main aim is to be authentic. If the question 'what should I be doing with my hands?' is on your mind, it simply shows that you are not actually fully present but worrying about how you come across, adding extra nerves. Whilst this is a very natural thought when starting out, it also gets into your head and out of your natural flow. You might be a more introverted speaker feeling uncomfortable with using extensive hand gestures – please do what feels natural to you to begin with, then add the various gestures for effect.

The better you know and have internalised your content, the easier it will be to give the element of body language more attention. When presenting new content, we are naturally more in our heads, retrieving from memory. On those occasions, learned hand gestures can distract from the authenticity of your content. Have you ever seen a speaker who seemed a bit robotic? This is typically because the hand gestures they are using are learned and don't come across naturally.

In summary, when presenting new content don't focus too intensely on your body language as you might come across as incongruent and that is the last thing you want when selling your ideas to an audience. Work on your grounding and ability to deal with nerves first before adding additional forms of delivery to your speaking.

Action Steps: body language

1. Film yourself when rehearsing your next talk or presentation.
2. Watch yourself back and observe what your hands and the rest of the body are doing.
3. Decide on a comfortable position for your arms and hands you can naturally fall back to in between gesturing with your hands.

Kelly's story

When talking about vulnerability and overcoming nerves, Kelly Pietrangeli comes to mind. Kelly is the creator of Project Me, a hub of resources and inspiration to help make life easier for busy mothers. Kelly has an amazing online profile, thousands of followers and loves connecting with her audience online. When she was asked to speak to a live audience at the Festival of Doers conference in London, she nearly turned it down as her online confidence didn't translate into standing before a live audience. Not wanting to miss the opportunity, she turned to Speaker Express and tackled her nerves head on. While working with us, she gave herself permission to drop perfection and simply be herself. She learned how to find her flow while remaining structured. Kelly began to speak not only with confidence but with power. One week before the big Festival of Doers conference, Kelly gave a speech at her own book launch that came from the heart. The response was so positive that she headed into the conference feeling nerves of excitement rather than sheer dread.

In a blog post that Kelly wrote on our website she shared her experience:

"When an audience member asked me a question I wasn't prepared for, I gave her an honest answer. I shared a very vulnerable story from my past that I'd barely told anyone before. The tears came and I didn't worry about looking unprofessional or feeling foolish. And when I left the stage a queue of women came to give me a hug, to thank me – and to buy copies of my book which had only just come out the week before.

I moved out of my comfort zone in a big way, and by doing so I've unlocked a part of me I hadn't even realised I'd been hiding away. I'm stepping into my power and I'm now organising my own all-day inspirational event, inviting speakers to share their stories and wisdom. I'll be on the stage several times throughout the day and I couldn't be more excited that I found my voice to share my stories.

'Stepping out of your comfort zone' may feel like an overused expression these days, but until you do it you won't know where it could lead and what opportunities and experiences you'll open yourself up for."

Four steps to mastering your confidence

Here is what Kelly did to overcome her challenge with public speaking and move forwards, and steps that you too could follow to take your confidence to the next level:

1. Take every chance to get on stage

Kelly took every chance to get on stage at the trainings. On one occasion, she signed up to do a five-minute talk at our Members' Impact Hour at 9am in the morning. The rule is, if you're late for your slot, you miss out on it – no exceptions. That morning when she got to the tube station, she discovered that her wallet was still at home and she couldn't get onto the train. It would have been easy to give up and go back home, but Kelly ran like Usain Bolt and made it to the venue with two minutes to spare to deliver her talk. It probably wasn't her best talk, but she knew that every opportunity to speak was going to make her better and she wasn't about to miss out.

2. Drop the script

When you retrieve your content from memory, your brain can go into overdrive and by trying to be too logical about the order of your script, you create more anxiety and block creativity.

At some point in time it will happen; you stand in front of your audience and totally lose your train of thought. It happened to

Kelly and yes it threw her as she was so attached to her script and getting it 'right'.

After that moment, Kelly learned the trick of taking a breath, looking at the audience and saying: "I want you to take a moment to think about what I just said." Pausing like this gives you time to slow down, but also helps your audience to digest your content. Then, continue with your flow. The more you speak, the more you'll learn how to internalise your material, allowing yourself to be more in the moment and present.

3. Allow yourself to be vulnerable

Kelly always thought speaking is about putting on a show, being the strong business woman who is teaching content to an audience. To be seen as the expert, she believed you have to be perfect. What she realised during the training and when speaking at the Festival of Doers is that an audience connects to you even more when you show them who you really are. By being vulnerable as a speaker, you show real strength.

4. Find your unique style

Kelly's experience is also a great example of how important is to find your unique style. Before I was interested in speaking myself, I would never pay any attention to how speakers came across or what methods they used. Soon after attending my first speaker training however, I became a keen observer, often falling in the 'compare to despair' trap. If you have never heard that expression, it means that you measure yourself against others in a negative way. You watch everyone else, putting them on a pedestal and putting yourself down; not a good way of learning. You tend to say to yourself, "They are so good – how will I get to be as good as them?". Don't ever compare your progress, except for learning purposes to improve and empower yourself. What can really help is to realise you are not perfect now, but will continue to improve forever. There will always be someone ahead and behind you. Be your own measurement of success.

Whilst we can learn a lot and get inspired from watching other speakers, your professional speaking journey isn't about becoming Oprah, Steve Jobs or Tony Robbins. It's about letting your very own personality and expertise do the talking. That will make you unique and help people buy into you and your brand.

Finding your unique style requires honesty to yourself. If speaking isn't your favourite activity in the world, but you know it will help your business growth, you must understand one thing – some people naturally love anything related to being in the spotlight, while others don't. Personally, I love every second of being on stage; it energises me. But I know that other people, especially introverts, reach a state of total depletion after a gig or a day of training, and that's OK.

Be very honest and gentle on yourself. Is your goal to be a speaker or will you be someone using speaking as a tool for business growth? Either way is great. Don't beat yourself up if other colleagues or fellow business owners are getting paid gigs faster by using the processes outlined in this book. Go at your own pace. Don't compare, as it will slow your progress even further if your mind is hooked on everyone else 'being better'. It often simply boils down to your personality type. As introverts replenish their energy from being alone and extroverts get their energetic boosts from being with people, you must simply align your results with your energetic ability.

Action Steps: finding your unique style

Make a list of business, science or media personalities you like. Find them on Youtube and watch them speak.

Instead of comparing yourself to them, watch, observe, learn and ask:

1. What can I learn from this speaker?
2. What do they do well?
3. What exactly is it that makes him or her so good?
4. What part of their style would suit me too?

Use your public speaking notebook and start to take notes.

CHAPTER 7

The Speakers' Method: Your Brand Message

Picture this.

You are at Wembley. 20,000 people are waiting to hear you speak. But then suddenly, the event organiser comes up to you and says, "Sorry mate, you only have 20 seconds. Make them count." Suddenly, whatever you had planned for your talk, is cut right down. How do you make an impact in a very short space of time? How do you leave an impression that lasts? The answer to this is in your message. The very essence of what you stand for, when delivered well, can be very powerful.

Every business and brand must have a core message. Every visionary and influencer must have one. Having a clear core message is an essential step towards achieving a greater goal: the goal of becoming a respected and powerful brand. For a brand message to be effectively executed, it should weave through every product and / or service you provide, and all marketing comms, all containing the very essence of what your business is about.

In order to make an impact fast, your core message should hit the person listening so they have instant comprehension of who you are and what you stand for. Think about those 20 seconds now, do you have a message ready to go? A core message is an idea and/or belief that is tightly intertwined with the very spirit, essence and core values of your way of doing business and what you stand for.

This is essential for anyone using speaking, as well as for marketing purposes.

Here are some well-known examples, although note that these are extremely short and stripped down to an even simpler brand message in their public-facing marketing:

- Nike: Just do it.
- Salesforce: No software.
- Subway: Eat fresh.
- Adidas: Impossible is nothing.
- Walmart: Save money. Live better.
- Levi's: Quality never goes out of style.

If you don't already have your core message, here is a very simple way to discover it. You just need to:

- Know – what is your statement of expertise and how does it relate to your ideal client?
- Problem – what is the challenge/problem you solve for them?
- Solution – what is your unique solution?
- Results – what results do you get for your ideal client?

Write one sentence for each.

What is important is that it's written in a language that your ideal client can understand.

Action Step: Your brand message

Have a go now at writing your own according to the above structure, or if you have one already, rework it according to this structure and pretend you only have 20 seconds to get this across.

Your core message is an essential element of your speaking toolkit and your business. Key messages are important because they are a huge part of effective communication. They convey what you, your business, your brand stand for in terms of impact. It's what you want others to know and remember. Most successful key messages are direct, short, to the point and must be interesting.

This structure has been used by various companies that we have worked with to centralise their marketing messaging and create consistency when they have multiple people selling their products. We have clients who go and rework all their marketing assets as a result of this. It is so important that your core message runs through all your communication, not just public speaking.

Here is an example or our core message, using this format:

Know – *Here, at Speaker Express we know that business owners and entrepreneurs are leaving money on the table by not using public speaking as a growth strategy.*

Problem – *The problem is that they don't know how to speak effectively or how it fits into their business strategy. Or when they do speak, they do a poor job of it, yielding little results.*

Solution – *The solution is our Speakers' Method…*

Results – *This results in business owners and entrepreneurs attracting qualified leads, growing their business and becoming the authorities and go-to experts in their industries.*

I hope this example demonstrates how simply you can articulate your brand message in a powerful manner so people understand what you do very quickly. This brand message is something you must have completely clear when presenting your brand on stage, and will form the foundation for your talks and content.

Brand story

Your brand story is very powerful, as is your personal story. In the world of business, the two are very much connected. The Speakers' Method is designed to help you share your story.

This includes different aspects of your personal and brand story, such as:

- How did you get started?
- What do you stand for?
- How will you create impact?

When you learn to enrol your ideal clients and audiences through stories, watch how your brand's reach extends and you have more impact. Stories also lead people to buying into you and what you stand for. The '5 stories every entrepreneur needs to tell' are covered in the signature talk chapter later on, so we will come back to this shortly.

Now, let's get back to Wembley with those 20,000 people waiting to hear what you say... and, go!

CHAPTER 8

The Speakers' Method: Your Signature Talk

> *To become a speaker in-demand you require at least one great speech and a clever profile-building strategy*

Having one, or a selection, of key talks that centre around your brand message will mark you out as the expert in your space and market. You will get known for a certain topic, enabling you to become a thought leader and the 'go to' person in your field.

Some people have 'the one' talk. However, with the content-rich culture we are now living in, people are demanding new material all the time, so whilst you might have your one preferred talk, it is best to have a selection of topics within your expertise that you can cover. We recommend you have at least 3–5 talks ready to go, all with content centring around your brand message. This will become your collection of signature talks and will make it easier for you to get booked, as you're more likely to have a talk that fits with what a booker is looking for. For example, here are the different topics that I speak on with regards to public speaking:

- How to Fall in Love with Public Speaking.
- How To Use Public Speaking To Grow Your Business.
- How to Get Booked Solid.
- The Truth About Building A Speaking Business.
- The Perfect Pitch.
- How to Sell from Stage.

As there are two of us representing Speaker Express, we have more than 5 between us. However, each one of these is a signature talk in its own right that we can deliver and adapt to suit the different audiences.

If you are just starting out, start with just one. Then, once you have achieved a high standard of excellence, add another. Bear in mind that not every talk you design is going to be a signature talk: you will simply add it to your toolbox of talks. We regularly help our clients to achieve this, so know it is a tried and tested strategy.

Each talk should be designed in a way that you can adapt according to your audience, time slot and what event organisers ask you to do. For example, my talk on 'The Perfect Pitch' could be delivered in more of a workshop format over a couple of hours, or a quick 10-minute presentation. Ultimately, you want to aim to have this amount of flexibility with each of your signature talks.

Structuring your Signature Talk

Every time you get the chance to step in front of an audience, your goal should be to leave them better off after hearing you speak.

We have a 7-step structure you can use to create any one of your key talks. This is a tried and tested framework, designed to give you strong positioning on stage, engage the audience through storytelling, and lead to sales and business growth. The seven steps are:

1. OPENING – finding a powerful way to grab the audience's attention from the get-go.
2. PROBLEM – how does your product or service solve a problem your audience/ideal client has?

3. EARN THE RIGHT – what gives you the right to speak on the subject matter?
4. SOLUTION – how do you solve your audience's problem?
5. STORY – a selected story that is relevant to the talk you are delivering.
6. EXPAND – go deeper into your solution and methodology.
7. CALL TO ACTION – what do you want the audience to do next?

Before going through these steps one by one, it's important to first think about the intention of your talk. Behind every talk, define the outcome and the reason for delivering it. Don't just step on stage because you have a product to sell, also think about the value you will offer. For example, is it to:

- Educate;
- Inform;
- Inspire action;
- Entertain;
- Persuade;
- Start a debate;
- Sell – although remember you are always selling, even when not directly;
- Motivate;
- A mix of some of those?

Your business reasons for stepping on stage could be:

- Growing your list.
- Promoting a new project.
- Fundraising for charity.
- Selling your products or services.
- Raising brand awareness.
- Enrolling people into a new school of thought.
- Raising investment.

We'll now go through each of the Signature Talk steps:

1. OPENING – 7 compelling ways to open a speech

You don't know what's going on in the lives of your audience and what is likely to distract them, so grabbing their attention from the get-go, making them forget their worries in your presence, would be great, right?

I'll go through some examples of how you can powerfully open a speech. Personally, I am a big fan of making the audience laugh. But, you need to ensure that everything you say suits your style. Seeing a speaker doing things that aren't comfortable to them can be painful. If you've ever seen someone awkwardly trying to tell a joke on stage, you'll know what I mean!

Here are various ways you can open your talk in an interesting way to draw your audience in. Remember to think about your personality type and choose what fits you, as not all of these will work for everyone:

- A personal story that demonstrates your connection to the topic in an authentic way.
- Something cheeky. You could start with: "I shouldn't be telling you this but..." to draw people in and create intrigue, as if you are about to let them in on a secret. This gets people to really listen. If you are using this opening though, you had better follow this up with telling them something unique and outstanding to have the desired effect.
- A question that you know appeals to them and will hook them in, such as "How many of you would like to learn how to generate leads on Linkedin?"
- A powerful statement, e.g. "We are heading for a global meltdown if something doesn't change quick."
- A joke, if humour is your thing.
- An interesting or shocking statistic.

- Simply pause and connect with the audience for a second or two. Use your presence to capture everyone's attention.

There are countless other ways you could open and multiple variations of those listed, all depending on your speaking style and the occasion, but the above will give you a good starting point for inspiration and get you thinking what could work for you.

Stage time is a gift, from you to your audience, and these examples will help to wrap your gift well to start with.

Action Step: Finding an opening

- Watch the first 10-15 seconds of a variety of different TED or TEDx talks. You can simply go to YouTube or ted.com and pick a random selection of talks that are more related to your business and field.
- Observe the openings the speakers use, making notes of those you find most compelling and why.
- How can you take inspiration from the openings you thought work best, and translate these into an opening for your own talk? Note down some ideas.

---

2. PROBLEM - What problem are you solving?

People in modern society tend to feel that they are short on time; we are moving faster and people are getting less patient. The likelihood is therefore that your audience will feel this way. This is why it is important that you very quickly assure the audience that they are in the right place and listening to you will be a valuable use of their time, by demonstrating that you know their problem.

People would have come to see you because in some way they believe, at least from the marketing or hearing about you, that you can solve their problem. They will be hoping that your talk will shed some light and help them find a way forwards with a solution because you can demonstrate an in-depth understanding of what keeps them up at night. This is true regardless of the sector you operate in. People want results from your service or product but first they want to know that you get them and understand their problem.

Imagine you showed up to one of my talks about how to use public speaking to grow your business and I didn't demonstrate that I understood your challenges first and jumped straight to solutions, how would you feel about spending money with me? Would you trust me? Would you feel like we understand you as a company? Would you believe that our solution is any good for you? The answer is probably not. People need to be shown first that you get them, you get their challenge and that you can explain it back to them.

By communicating the problem early on it displays authority and expertise, uncovering the pain of the audience and helping them see that you understand what 'keeps them awake at night'. That assures them that spending the time listening to you is the right thing to do.

Action Step: what problem are you solving?

Take a minute to answer these questions to clearly define the problem you are addressing and why and how you are addressing it.

- Does the problem you solve exist on a global scale? Or is it a local issue? Is it online/offline?
- What is unique about your solution that people want to hear you speak about?
- Why do you care?
- Why are you the person to listen to on the issue?
- How will their lives be better after using your product or service?

3. EARN THE RIGHT - Demonstrate your credibility

Assuming that you have caught the audience's attention (opening) and that you have shown to your audience that you get their problem, they will then think who are you and why you? Why should the audience listen to what you have to say?

This is where you introduce your credentials which we refer to as ETR – Earn The Right. Getting on stage is something that you earn, it is not an entitlement. By standing there and listing your credentials, you are earning your right to talk about the topic and giving the audience a reason to listen to you and value your opinion.

When adding in your ETR think about your credibility to speak on this topic; why should they listen to and trust you on this? You can include your biggest achievements, years of experience and expertise, publications, awards, years spent in certain industries, academic achievements, names of big clients, hours of coaching expertise, degrees or PhDs, etc.

For those at the beginning, walking away from something is equally as credible, e.g. "I was a lawyer for 25 years and walked away to dedicate my life to XYZ." You can also talk about your personal passion and your 'why' here, such as being a parent, having suffered from an illness, etc. E.g. "After beating cancer twice, I was determined to find significant healthier options for my lifestyle and share those with others."

Action Step: ETR

Write down a list of all your accomplishments and experiences that make you an expert on your topic.

4. SOLUTION – How do you solve the problem?

In this part of your talk, you demonstrate your solution to the predefined problem:

- What is your unique system?
- Your unique service?
- Your unique product?

Like any of the sections in the Signature Talk, this is to show that you not only get their problem but you have the solution for it too. People buy results while looking for compassion and someone who understands their problem. The sooner you can demonstrate your solution the quicker people buy into you, your brand and your offering.

You don't have to give everything away at this point, simply demonstrate you have a solution and it is the right one (the expansion and delving into your content comes later in Step 6).

It is important that whatever your solution is, it is presented as unique and different or you will come across as vanilla, and you don't want people thinking 'I know that'. It is also important that it is easy to understand – too complex and the computer says no.

Really take time to think of the visual aspect of presenting your solution – the look and how people feel when they see it. Keep it simple, yet insightful.

5. STORY: Telling a story to enhance your credibility and captivate the audience

As a speaker, it's not only about delivery, tools and structure. Having all the tools in place will give you the confidence to get out there, but it doesn't differentiate you from anybody else. Your personal story goes a long way towards setting you apart from other speakers. Not only because your story is unique to you, but also because it creates a great level of rapport and connection.

All too often, we undervalue the power of our own stories. Saying that, I am sure you have sat through talks where the speaker went on and on and on about themselves, or a talk that left you wondering, 'who is this person I am listening to?' When it comes to using your personal background and story it's all about balance. One thing I can promise you though is, if done right, it will enhance your credibility and connection with the audience.

There are many ways you can weave storytelling into your talk. Here, I will talk through five types of stories that are a great starting point.

The 5 Stories Every Entrepreneur Needs To Know How To Tell:

1. Your vision – how you are creating transformation: 'Imagine a world where…'

Last week, I bought a ticket for a flight to Berlin. I didn't buy the plane. I bought the **destination**. Too many entrepreneurs spend time describing in detail how they are going to deliver their solution. That's called selling the plane. Sell the destination. What results and transformation do you want to achieve in the world?

Here is ours:

To be a leading public speaking training company globally for entrepreneurs who love solving meaningful problems, want to get their message out there, grow their businesses and make more impact.

Being able to communicate all these elements and spread your story makes your brand relatable, personable and is what people will buy into.

2. Your personal story – how you've overcome obstacles and why you are qualified to help.

When it comes to the business of persuasion and influence, remember this simple but powerful equation: Motivation = Inspiration. If you want to attract your ideal clients and inspire them to take action, it's critical that you share the reason you got into this business in the first place. By sharing your story you demonstrate first-hand experience around the pain point you're trying to solve for your client, establishing a powerful, authentic bond.

Here are some ways to use your personal story to inspire and create motivation in your audience:

- **Adversity** – sharing your deepest and darkest moment or experience from a healed place, which then inspired you to do what you do.
- **Growth story** – how you went from an idea to growing something special.
- **Innovation** – how you pioneered something new, the process of how you got there and the result you've achieved.

3. Your business origin story – how did you get started?

Tell the story of how you got started. Audiences love this. It connects and inspires.

4. Your credibility story – success stories/testimonials + overcoming objections.

Quite possibly the most misunderstood of all the entrepreneur stories. Your credibility story is not your experience or the titles you hold. It's about the results your clients have achieved, or the process/coaching/product by which you help your clients achieve those results. Have *at least* 5 testimonial stories under your hat.

5. Your sales / elevator pitch – the benefit of your work.

Here, you pitch your product, service and brand. While the whole signature talk is doing this in a way, this is the part where you would sell, show the features and benefits, key results they will get by choosing to buy from you, how they buy from you, the price. There are lots of different ways to structure these, which is why it has its own chapter later on.

Landing your story right

Make your stories and content newsworthy and interesting. Spend time thinking about who you are and what matters. This isn't about broadcasting your private life, but personalising your business life.

The way you communicate builds your credibility, but you must ensure that it is carefully crafted for the right audience. For example, I have a range of different stories that I use according to the audience I am speaking to, as well as the outcome I want at the end of our talk. I have a personal story about confidence; I have a story about how I got involved with Speaker Express; I have a story about my wife kicking my ass because I was too busy with work; I have a story about turning my business around from bankruptcy to success. I think you get the picture: ultimately the story must enhance your credibility as well as build rapport with the audience and relate to what you are selling at the end.

Sometimes a few sentences will be enough to give your audience the feeling they know you a bit better, and sometimes you will want to go a bit deeper with your story. It all depends on the event brief and why the audience is there in the first place. Make it relevant. If you are talking about time-management, bringing up your last holiday adventure on how you climbed Kilimanjaro isn't as relevant as your previous corporate background where you streamlined a global project and really got ahead by building personal relationships with the team. With the latter, you can build on and share your 3-step methodology on how to save time by having close relationships with the team.

Action Step: craft a story

Think of a personal moment in your life in relation to your business and craft a 5-minute story using any of the above structures.

---

6. EXPAND

This section is where you dive deeper into your content. Here you can show off your expertise and knowledge in your field, but also provide real value in business insights for your audience. Make sure your content has clear takeaways, results and insights. It works well for this expansion to build from the solution model you presented earlier in section 4 (Solution).

Remember, you want your audience to be finding your content in this part of your talk extremely valuable, to be grabbing a pen and paper to write down as much as they can.

7. CALL TO ACTION

Finishing with a strong next step will help to convert an opportunity into business. This part can be the most uncomfortable for many people but also the most important for your success as a speaker.

At times in the seminar world, there was a very successful strategy that some speakers in certain industries would use which was creating a sense of false scarcity – for example, an offer only available to the first 5 people, therefore encouraging people in the audience to run to the back of the room or to buy on the day before prices go up.

We believe that if you have a powerful proposition, providing real value and solving people's problems, there is no need to use dated sales techniques. People love buying stuff that solves their problems. They love moving forward with their lives and making progress. However, they don't want to be pushed into a decision before they've had the opportunity to learn, research and evaluate whether it fits their situation. Your job is to deliver an outstanding presentation that gets them to experience you and the value of your work, which in turn will get them to buy from you and your company.

To arrive at a solid call to action, go back to your intended outcome for your talk. The reason for your talk and where you are wanting to lead your audience must be crystal clear. If nobody does anything different than they would have done before you spoke, the value of your speech is zero.

Make sure the call to action is clear and concise, and don't task your audience with doing too many things. One action step for them, and one way they can connect or continue with you, works well.

Audience Psychology: The silent questions that go through your audience's mind

Every section in the Signature Talk structure is designed to enrol the audience into listening more and wanting to buy from you. It is therefore important to understand the audience psychology and how to manage it.

Even if you have someone introducing you and they do a great job, there are four subconscious questions that go through the mind of your audience when you start your talk:

Who are you? – People want to very quickly know about you and what your credibility is for standing there and talking about your subject. This is why we include the step 'Earn The Right' early on, allowing your audience to hear all about what qualifies you to stand in front of them. This isn't about showing off. It simply demonstrates to the audience that you have a right to stand there and speak.

Why should I care? – This is the next question that goes through people's minds, and it is a great question. You must therefore demonstrate very quickly what you will be addressing in your talk and why it is something that the audience will want to know about.

Do I trust you? – This is a natural question to be going through anyone's mind if they don't know you yet. You actually spend most of a talk winning the audience's trust, but you can start to win it very quickly by bringing in a bit of your story, be it personal or about your business. Remember: people buy from people, and normally from people they like. We always get asked how much of your personal story you should share. The answer isn't straightforward: it depends. Some of the people we train put a lot of their personal story into their introduction because it relates to the services they offer, whereas for others in might not. If you are a personal brand, your personal story is likely to be very relevant.

Some talk about their passion, which is why they built their business the way they did and some people insert how they got to where they are today. The key is to be authentic and real. Remember everything counts, and these days a simple Google search can reveal any holes.

One of our members, Angela, is a food entrepreneur and chef who, when she joined us, was invited to do a talk for her industry. When it came to this part, she wasn't sure how her personal story was relevant. We worked on it and came up with a format that gave enough of her story without getting too personal.

After she had given her first talk, she told us: *"I went from thinking, 'I don't have a story' to speaking on the same stage as the Mayor of New*

York City and landing three additional international speaking engagements."

Angela won the audience over, and they trusted her because she was willing to show a little bit of her human side. Be brave, get vulnerable.

What's in it for me? – Also known as WIFM, the audience wants to know what they are going to get from the talk, and why they should invest their time listening to you. People are self-motivated and mostly only do things for themselves. You are reading this book because you want to learn how public speaking can be used as a tool in your business which will help you, right? It is the same when people attend your talk. They want to learn something which will give them the edge and you need to let them know upfront what it is they are going to gain from listening to you. Otherwise, they will check out.

Remember that the reason you are speaking is because you are an expert in your field and have something valuable to offer. Never apologise for standing up for what you are talking about. Never start a talk with an apology as it puts your audience in an uncomfortable place.

Here are some other common mistakes for you to avoid:

- Using alienating language or language that is not relevant to the audience. For example: "Today I am going to talk about the accounting legislation which affects house buying for HMOs" when the audience is there to learn how to buy their first house.
- Being self-indulgent and talking too much about yourself.
- Using content or stats that are irrelevant. For example, mentioning a Martin Luther King speech when the topic is about being vegan.
- Over-running or using too much 'fluff', i.e. highly intangible and airy fairy content.

- Using too much text or images that are irrelevant on slides.
- Spending most of the presentation looking at/reading the slides.
- Ignoring the audience.
- Over-justifying yourself and why you are on stage.
- Continuously stating that you are not a speaker.
- Looking down.
- Rocking backwards, forwards, crossing your legs while standing and speaking.
- Using generalisations such as: "everybody wants", "everyone here", "you all".

Reading the room

With experience comes the ability to read the energy of the audience. This isn't hocus pocus, this is a very important aspect for anyone using public speaking. It's the ability to sense how the audience is responding to your content and having the flexibility to adapt accordingly.

Reading the room is how you can manage the audience to ensure that they get maximum value from hearing your talk while you remain fully in control. It's seeing how everything is landing, and how your content is being received. It's about knowing that if someone has raised a point that might contradict yours or challenge you, you will know how to manage it. It's how you deal with that one person who isn't interested in hearing what you have to say. To do this takes strength not to let your insecurities take over, and instead having unshakable inner confidence to remain in control.

To give you an example of this, I was once doing one of my seminars and everyone seemed to be having a great time. At the time, I was a little inexperienced. At one point in the seminar, I went into my sales pitch and because I didn't know how to read the audience well, at the end of the sales pitch, the audience was ready to jump me. Some people were sitting back, looking angry; others were looking away. In fact, I had lost them completely. When I picked up on this, I immediately asked them what was wrong? The answer I got shocked me. It wasn't that they minded being sold to, it was how I went from supportive to salesy. Luckily, I was able to win them back over by being myself again and actually got some sales from it. However, if I had been able to read the audience better, I would have changed tack and approach much earlier.

The more alert you are to reading the audience, the quicker you will be able to adapt. Some things to look out for while delivering are:

- Normally your gut can sense the room – listen to it.
- Watch for people's facial expressions.
- Body language such as crossing arms, looking out of the window, shaking heads, leaning back from you.
- Slouching.
- Looking at the phones or starting to talk amongst themselves.

Some people can do this very naturally, while for others it takes time. However, developing your speaker audience awareness is a must; a bit like having a superpower.

We share many more tips on the blog page of our website, so make sure to check it out:
https://www.speakerexpress.co.uk/blog/

CHAPTER 9

The Speakers' Method: Getting Booked

The question I get asked more than any other is: "How do I get more speaking gigs?" This is a fundamental part of The Speakers' Method. There is no point in you being confident with great talks without any knowledge on how to get booked as a speaker.

It goes without saying that until you reach a certain level, you will have to do a lot of self-promotion. This part of the Speakers' Method is all about how to do this: from who to contact to having a solid showreel, to having a speaker sheet and knowing how to pitch yourself. A lot of speakers simply don't know how to get themselves on stage. There are various ways to do it, which are covered in this chapter.

Pitching yourself to get booked

If you want to get on stage more often, there is a 'secret ingredient' – something many people know, but few implement. The secret ingredient is: TO ASK! Start creating opportunities. Being proactive and taking action to expand your circle of influence is the way to go.

Research the groups and events that your potential clients go to. In your city there are so many regular meetings, conferences, talks, workshops, lunches, breakfasts, evening events, webinars, break-out sessions and more. They all want valuable content for their community members or conference attendees. Yes, at times you will get rejected, but it won't kill you! I promise, wink wink.

One of our clients was terrified of putting herself out there. In order to overcome this fear, she deliberately started with getting comfortable when rejected. You might even want to set yourself a target to get 10 rejections the day you are contacting people. You will soon find out your conversion ratio – how many people do you have to speak to before you get a booking? Maybe you talk to 10 people: 9 say "no", one says "yes".

This is a script we are happy to share with you. While it is designed for emails, it also works for phone calls. Try using the script below and see what happens:

Dear…

Add something which personalises your message (check their LinkedIn or Facebook posts for inspiration).

I just wanted to know what you would need from me to have a conversation about being a speaker at your next event? I am a huge fan of your events.

I am more than happy to jump on Zoom/Skype or meet you for a coffee to discuss.

Please find attached my speaker sheet and my link to my showreel.

Thank you in advance

Name

If you don't ask closed questions, it's unlikely to get a direct 'NO' that can really hurt. Instead, you are starting a conversation and a relationship with the person responsible for booking speakers.

How to get started (14 spaces to get booked in London)

There are an overwhelming number of potential clients for you out there, and so many different stages/events/conferences to reach them. Saying that, deciding which stages to speak on and who to approach is an art in itself.

If you are a complete novice, you may be wanting to play it safe. If so, check out storytelling platforms in your area.

Speaking platforms in London to get you started:

Inspire'd Stage. One of my favourite places – this is an inspiring story-based community that runs events in Mayfair in the basement of a beautiful pub. It's very much about your raw stories. As a speaker on the Inspire'd Stage, you share your story in an authentic and vulnerable way. They also film your speaking performance, so you can spot opportunities to improve. If your video is really good, they will publish it and you can probably pay for your recording. Inspire'd Stage is definitely a platform worth checking out, particularly because Shay, one of the founders, has such charisma on stage and a big heart.

The College of Public Speaking. Every year they run a competition called *The Corporate Challenge*, which I would recommend for seasoned speakers and newbies alike. The Corporate Challenge is all about creating a seven-minute talk and the event is filmed. There are two different heats, made up of 10 people in each heat. If you're awesome and amazing, you'll get through to the final. Last year, Jackie, a Speaker Express member, joined and finished in third place. If you'd like to step up to The Corporate Challenge, get in touch with Vince and Michael from The College of Public Speaking who run it.

FuckUp Nights. They run events at The Hub in King's Cross and they really love having entrepreneurs; business owners who are happy to share their fuck-ups. If you haven't screwed up in your business, what are you doing? You're clearly playing it too safe!

Moth Storytelling. Originated in New York, now in London. They hold all sorts of live events including StorySLAM; an open mic' storytelling competition and have a global community of storytellers.

Spark London. A storytelling club which holds events in London and Glasgow. The rule here is for participants to tell personal stories on condition that they are true and can be told in under 5 minutes.

Interesting Talks. The founder, Matt Kendall, has built this to be the biggest personal development Meet-up event in Europe. He's awesome when it comes to giving speakers a stage and you can connect with him in the Speaker Express Facebook Group. Like most event organisers, he can be really picky about who he chooses. However, if you follow what we teach in this book, I am sure you can charm him.

Here are some links if you'd like to find out more:

- www.stories.co.uk
- www.inspiredinlondon.com
- www.glugevents.com
- www.thestoryparty.co.uk
- www.fuckupnights.com/london
- www.uk.funzing.com
- www.hubdot.com
- www.nowjustaddwater.com
- www.naturalbornstorytellers.com
- www.themoth.org
- www.thecavendisharmsstockwell.co.uk/comedy [open mic for comedy virgins]

Once you've got started, spend some time looking into which gigs generated the best leads/clients for you – clearly, those are the stages/event organisers with whom you want to develop a stronger relationship.

If you are already a seasoned speaker and you are looking for more specific business-related gigs, check out your local library or your local Chamber of Commerce.

Your footage and showreel

You can Google information about being a speaker, read about speaker sheets and see people's websites. However, you can't get a feeling from Google or any sheet for someone's style or authenticity. Quality footage is crucial if you want to be a paid speaker.

We get a lot of enquiries from corporates asking for people who speak on various subjects such as nutrition, wellbeing, creativity, resilience, sales, remote working, etc. To be considered as a serious contender for speaking gigs, corporates will require you to have a video of you speaking. Not, "Erm, I'm doing a Facebook Live," but in front of a real audience.

The more you speak, the more opportunity you have to capture footage. The more you do this, the more you should invest in a professional camera and mic. People are very forgiving these days in terms of video; no longer do we need the extravagant studio. However, when it comes to sound quality, we are not so forgiving and it needs to be clearly audible.

Therefore, when you speak, capture as much of it as you can, as later you can use it for your showreel which can be sent out to get you more speaking gigs and raise your profile. This is a must if you want to stand out.

Here is what you must include in your showreel and how to structure it:

- Your expertise – must come across in the first few seconds, as the person who might book you wants to know that you are a leader in your field. Having someone introduce you onto the stage is always a good way to demonstrate this.
- Display the problem you are solving and how you are making an impact.

- Highlights of content – capture the key moments in your talk, and the key aspects of your presentation. Really display what's in it for your audience.
- Let your personality come through – content, stories, moments of wisdom, interesting statistics, great quotes.
- Include testimonials.
- Include impressive clients.
- Have a strong ending.
- Make sure people know how to contact you.

Here are some more tips to consider:

- Keep it short: around 90-150 seconds.
- If you are using music, make sure it doesn't sound cheap or overpower you.
- Make it specific to the people who you want to book you and for the intended audience.
- Don't repeat footage.
- Make sure it displays energy (no one likes a boring speaker).
- Make sure it looks professional.

For a comprehensive guide to your showreel, we have an example on our website. Go https://www.speakerexpress.co.uk/elliot-kay/ if you would like to see more.

Preparing your media pack

To get your business or product featured in a major publication is great. Imagine the largest publication in your industry or even a local news affiliate giving you free press. Now imagine the kind of exposure and traffic this would bring to your business. Even better, imagine that your favourite journalist just got in touch and wanted you to send over everything they need to do a feature on you. They want your best image, bio and to get a feel for you and your brand. That is where your media pack comes in. Think of it as everything in one place. A one-stop shop. One email sent or one link and they have everything. You don't have to start with this, but having it will certainly help and show you are a professional.

Everything above applies even if you are simply looking to get booked, regardless of journalists or not. I run conferences and events all the time and I am always on the look-out for great speakers. Recently, I ran a conference and asked speakers to submit an application form and out of the 50 applications, only three had showreels and media packs – it shows you how easy it is to stand out because so few people do the basics.

What are speaker agents looking for?

To demonstrate what speaker agents look for, I thought it would be best to take some key highlights from an interview we did with Maria Franzoni who runs a very successful speaker bureau, Maria Franzoni Ltd, and has worked with incredible speakers such as Richard Branson, Neil Armstrong, Steve Wozniak, and Liza Minnelli, to name but a few. She's also the founding member of the European Association of Speakers' Bureaus and she was head judge at our female speakers' conference awards earlier this year.

Annik: Let's talk about speaker bureaus: what does a speaker bureau actually do, how do they work with their clients and, most importantly, how do they differ to a speaker agent?

Maria: I think until you're in the world of speaking and until you've actually dealt with speaker bureaus, you probably have no idea that we exist and I didn't know about speaker bureaus at all until I started working for one.

A speaker bureau is a resource for clients who are running conferences, events, masterclasses, looking for some expertise in some shape or form. We serve the client. Even though we call ourselves a "speaker bureau", we serve the client requiring the expert or the speaker. Normally, that client would come to us and say, "This is my requirement, this is what I want to achieve," and they would ask us for our guidance and advice because it's our job to know who the top people are in the field out there delivering – who's current, who's hot.

What's the difference between the bureau and an agent? A bureau would have a huge number of speakers on their books and they don't answer to the speaker in terms of the business they bring. They answer to the client and serve the client. They obviously look after the speaker, support the speaker but an agent actually supports the speaker. An agent is there to help a speaker with their business and make sure they have enough work. Whether it's TV or whether it's speaking or whatever it happens to be. With these different focuses, the focus of the bureau is with the client, providing them with speaker expertise. The focus of the agent is looking after the talent, so it's the other side.

Annik: *At Speaker Express, we work with a lot of up-and-coming speakers and often I hear them saying, "Oh, I wish I would find an agent, then my marketing would be sorted. I don't have to look for gigs and do all the really difficult business side of it – just rock up and speak."*

Maria: *That's the ideal world, but there's very few agents that would take somebody on unless they're already established to a certain degree. Bureaus aren't usually interested in beginners. We aren't interested in newbies unless it's somebody who just stepped down as a CEO of a big brand or has just done something like cross the Atlantic single-handedly, or whatever they might have done. Then it's a story and then they don't have to have speaking experience because it's what they've done that makes them relevant and current.*

Agents really want people who already have some kind of established career and they want to take them to the next level. There are some agents who would work with a beginner. But usually I think – and I'm not an expert in this area – you probably have to pay those people to do that rather than them take cuts of your bookings. Normally, a bureau or an agent will take a percentage of what they get you. Somebody who has to do all that marketing or all that work if you are starting out will probably charge you to do that. It's a different model.

Annik: *I feel like I'm liking the digging today. I'm going to dig a bit more. What are some unique traits you have seen? You know where maybe you have signed someone new and you liked them because of that unique trait. What are some things that really make speakers stand out?*

Maria: *Let me give you a wonderful example that I love. There are speakers that I book a lot because they are unique and because they're memorable. When I describe them to a client, the client gets excited because they see and hear how unique they are too.*

For example, a lot of clients have issues with communication and negotiation in particular. So, there's a lot of different speakers that you can recommend on those two subjects. Here's one that you'll never forget. You don't even need to know his name because you will describe him as I describe him and then anybody who's in the bureau will know who that is.

Negotiation. A former hostage negotiator who in his session re-enacts the hostage situation where the most senior person is taken hostage by one of his colleagues and gets the audience to negotiate the hostage's freedom. Now, you'll never forget that.

Annik: *Apart from the footage, what are perhaps some of the lesser-known insider criteria as you choose speakers?*

Maria: *Again, it depends who the target audience is, but referrals are great. If somebody is saying this speaker was great. I love it when a client does this… though not when another speaker refers a speaker. That, unfortunately, doesn't carry the same weight for me because a speaker recommending another speaker hasn't actually put their hand in their pocket and paid that speaker. But, if a client says to me, "Look, last year we had…"*

Often, a new client comes to us and we ask, "Who did you have last year? Who did you book them through? Why did you come to me?" They might say, "We have this person. Absolutely fantastic. We sourced him ourselves." Or whatever.

I will always go and check that person out and have a look. That's often how I recruit people. Because if my client is buying somebody, I know they're telling me that they're good and they delivered. That's probably a lesser-known way.

> **To listen to the full podcast, you can go here:**
> **https://tinyurl.com/stgpodcast**

What's in it for people booking you?

I have personally, before Speaker Express, been in the game for over a decade now with running various businesses, and I can't tell you how many times I hear the following things from people who want to speak on stage:

- "I have written a book and am looking to promote it."
- "I am a speaker, can I speak on your stage?"
- "You should book me because I am a good speaker."
- "I am sending this email to let you know that I am in your country and happy to speak for you."

While these are all relevant for the people who approach us, it means little to us and it tells us little as to why we should put them on stage – which is why they are usually met with a big fat, "No!"

If you want to ensure that you get booked for the right reasons, here are some keys that will help you with that:

- What will the audience gain?
- What is it that makes you unique?
- Who is your talk ideally for?
- How will what you speak about add value to the audience? (Show that you really care about them).

- What will you bring to the table in terms of helping to promote/sell tickets?
- How big is your social media presence?
- Will you be teaching something new?
- How will the audience feel?
- What will you be selling?
- Do you sell?
- What's your track record?

You must also be able to communicate the results you have had from people that have heard you speak:

- How did your talk impact them?
- Because of your talk and business growth, were you able to serve and impact a worthy cause?
- How is what you are doing creating an impact?
- How are you disrupting (if that's what your company is doing)?
- What have you pioneered?

Remember that while people buy from people, when you get on stage it's *results* that events bookers love. To sell yourself as a speaker, the results you bring to the table and your ability to communicate them, is essential.

SO HOW DO I GET MORE SPEAKING GIGS?

Back to THE question I hear most often from speakers (aspiring and professional ones): "HOW DO I GET MORE SPEAKING GIGS?" (or "How do I get started with speaking gigs?")

Most big cities (including London) are FULL of opportunities and if you wanted to, you could speak around the clock, seven days a week. Yet, despite this, most speakers struggle just because they have no idea how to make an approach and what to say.

When it comes to getting booked, it's all about connecting with the right people and building that network. This little 'finding gigs sequence' as we like to call it, can make all the difference to the number of your bookings. It will help you get into the speaking circuit. Follow these steps to get started:

1. Research – look at who you need to connect with, find out about them, look for ways to build rapport.
2. Connect – reach out to them, be polite and respectful, and come from a space of adding value.
3. Nurture – work on the relationship, do things to help them out, help them make useful connections (sending chocolate brownies is always a good move).
4. Follow up – stay in touch as "not now" or "not this time" doesn't mean "no" forever. Keep reminding them that you are there.
5. Get booked.

Start by spending at least 30 minutes a week applying the above sequence to get yourself booked for gigs.

Other avenues to get booked:

- Chamber of Commerce.
- Banks with a business team that runs events.
- Libraries that run business events.
- Check out other speakers that speak on your topic or complementary subjects and contact the event organisers.
- Go through Eventbrite to find organisers.

The bigger gigs will follow once you have built up enough credibility and expertise at ground level.

No more, *"I don't know where to start."* I'm afraid this isn't a good enough excuse any more. Start to do something by simply following the above sequence for a minimum of 30 minutes per week (or per day).

James's story

James Pattison runs a few businesses. When he joined us, he had set up a new company that lends money to start-ups. At the time, it was started in close connection to Dragons' Den.

James was not a fan of speaking, but as he constantly found himself in those situations, he knew something needed to change. James came to us and started to work on his speaking. He would show up, work hard, take in the trainings and apply them right away. He then formed partnerships with co-working spaces, speaking for free about his services while integrating the use of stories. His business grew fast as a result and they opened two more branches across the UK.

Recently, I saw James speak at a funding-related multi-speaker event and it struck me how much James stood out as he used portions of his own entrepreneurial journey and linked these back to relevant business points for his audience. In the 15 minutes he spoke, you could get a sense of the person running this business. The audience could relate to him, and his business did well as a result.

CHAPTER 10

The Speakers' Method: Pitch and Sales

> *Get into the mindset that whenever you get on stage, you are selling. You are selling yourself, your brand, your business, your vision, your values, your products/services and a cause you might believe in.*

This part is all about monetising your speaking. We'll be answering these pressing questions:

- How do you charge?
- How do you utilise speaking to gain more sales leads?
- How do you sell from stage in a way that is real to you and authentic to your brand and company values?
- How do you make sure that you are giving just the right amount of personal story with content that will urge people to buy into you as a brand and as a person?

Learning how to monetise your speaking and how to sell is one of the greatest skills you can gain. We want to give you a simple tool to determine if you should take a speaking opportunity or not, and for that you need to follow the 3 F's: Fee, Free or Flee.

To make sure you maximize on the opportunity, consider the 3 F's.

Fee – This means you get paid for your talk. A fee is agreed upfront for your time and contribution. Whilst you are still promoting yourself and your brand etc., you likely won't be selling a physical product or service on the night, as you are already being paid for your time by the organiser. The fees can vary dramatically from £50 to tens of thousands, depending on the size of event and level of your expertise/experience.

Free – you will often be asked to speak for free, and that's absolutely fine as long as there is a fair exchange in terms of you being able to sell, promote or gain leads from the event (sometimes known as "skimming" the room in promoter lingo).

Flee – if you can't sell and there is no budget to pay you, then you are simply speaking for the sake of speaking. Unless you are gaining experience, we recommend that you flee. If you are a beginner and looking to gain confidence, you may want to accept these gigs as practice and a space to speak with no pressure.

In other words, if the main person gaining from you speaking is the organiser, then flee from the opportunity. I know that this might sound hard, however you must consider how much you value your time and expertise. It's also harder to charge for one event when you speak for free at others.

Having the confidence to sell

It all starts with the simple notion: believe in yourself and your proposition.

Let me ask you a question. If you had the cure for the deadliest disease, would you hold back from shouting about it? Would you let your nerves or fears get in the way? Would you let other people's judgment of you stop you? Or would you shout it from the rooftops? Would you post about it on social media and make sure that everyone knew about it?

Now, some people have that sense of urgency and conviction when promoting their business and brand. However, when it comes to public speaking, they suddenly throw all that confidence out of the window and become a shadow of themselves. The amount of times I have met powerful people that are self assured in one-to-one settings, but when it comes to putting themselves in front of an audience, they fall apart, therefore losing potential business and opportunities.

To sell authentically on stage, it is important that your self-belief be unshakeable. Belief comes from the inside and shines on the outside. If you don't believe in your abilities, then no one will; sad but true. Mastering self-belief as a speaker influences all other areas of life. Because of this, when starting out public speaking, a lot of our clients end up on a personal development journey, and building their confidence on stage links in to other areas of their life.

I am making a bold assumption that you believe in your brand and business, and there is a reason you have made it this far. The same certainty in your message must come across when you pitch your product or service. Remember the results you have achieved and how much your solution can help people in the audience, and come from that space. Believing that you have "the cure" is crucial, and the first element of selling from stage.

Making friends with money

I find it fascinating how speaking can be such a metaphor for our life and how adding public speaking as a practice can expose and reveal a lot about us and our beliefs. Our mindset and psychology underpins our confidence and authenticity on stage. If you have a conflicted relationship with money, you will get in your own way when it comes to pitching and selling.

We all have different relationships with money. For many, it is a source of pain. It reminds us of what we don't have: the house, the car, the thriving business. For me, it used to represent what I didn't have, especially around Christmas time, I was always reminded what I couldn't afford and who wasn't in my life. On the other hand, for some us it is the greatest source of opportunity and gives us so much.

Our relationship with money evolves and changes at different times throughout our life. If you have trouble selling or pitching, I would encourage you to explore your relationship with money, as there could be an underlying issue getting in the way.

I have made a lot of money and I have lost a lot of money, and here is what I have found: the more you treat money with respect, the more it hangs around. The more you welcome money, nourish your relationship with it (or the energy of it), the more it sticks around. I find the level of people's ability to earn is a reflection of their relationship with money and their belief system around it. While you might be running a successful business right now, it is important that you always work on your relationship with money and keep nourishing it. This means that when you add speaking to your toolkit, you have to know your value, ask for it and charge accordingly.

I have found time and time again with people who run businesses, they might pull in great turnover and cash flow, but when it comes to self-worth on a personal level they struggle. Remember that what you will add by being on stage is worth every penny; always focus on the bigger picture and the value you are contributing.

If you want to read more about healing your relationship with money, here is a blog we wrote a few years back: https://www.speakerexpress.co.uk/i-love-sales/

Business models for speakers – nine ways to monetise your speaking

These nine different business models you can use to make money as a speaker will help you to understand a range of opportunities so that you can explore the right model for you.

When going through this list, think about where you are right now as a speaker and where you might want to progress. You may currently be speaking for free and considering your next step. Or you may be a more experienced speaker who wants to get better at converting or attracting prospects to your business.

It's not a complete list – there are hundreds of variations when it comes to using public speaking to push your career or grow your business. However, this list will give you a solid understanding of the available speaking models – whatever stage you're at.

1. Speaking for free

Taking on free speaking gigs is the best way to get started and there are many different platforms to do it on. When my co-founder, Annik, started out in 2011, the City Business Library was a great resource for her to perfect her speaking skills. They were looking for speakers to run small workshops for their business community and they still do this today. There are many other platforms that I recommend, as outlined in the previous chapter (Get Booked).

Note: If you're planning free speaking gigs, make sure that you have a clear agreement with the event organiser on how you can promote your product/service at the end of your talk, or do some list building by offering a free information product and collecting contact details.

2. Running events

If you're able to facilitate, have a network or are good at marketing, then putting on your own events is a great way to go. This approach helps you to build your profile, as people will come specifically to see you and you won't dilute your impact as you would if you shared the stage with other speakers. You can use your event to plug your unique products and services and make your attendees aware that the event is hosted by your brand.

3. Speaking at conferences

By dedicating some time to research online, you will discover conference speaking opportunities all over the world, in every industry. The process of becoming a speaker at a conference is generally straightforward; you apply and if you're liked, you'll get a "Yes" from the event organizer and then they'll fill the room for you. You don't even have to do any marketing – you just show up and speak!

A key part of your agreement is whether your speaking gig is paid or unpaid. If it's paid, the organisers will pay you to deliver your content or a keynote. If it's a free gig, make sure you agree terms that will benefit you, such as being able to sell your product, invite people to join your list or make an offer to attendees at the end of your talk. You may be able to have a table at the conference with your branding where people can come and connect with you throughout the event.

4. Keynote speaking

Keynote speaking is an option for more experienced speakers. Keynote speakers often work through a speaker bureau or employ a speaker agent and can make excellent money.

For example, if an organiser is planning a large sales conference, they'll contact different speaker bureaus and say, "We have a sales conference: who can do a 45-minute keynote on the power of sales?"

By getting a keynote speaking gig, you can expect to earn upwards of £500. Experienced speakers go in for £10,000 and celebrity speakers, like Anna Wintour, can command £100,000 plus.

Keynote speakers don't just fall out of the sky. They've typically spent years refining their content and their craft. They often speak on one of three key topics which are highly sought after in the corporate arena: resilience, creativity and future trends.

Resilience is a hot topic, as it's an essential skill for leaders to develop in challenging corporate environments. Creativity is also a popular topic, as corporations face the constant need to innovate. The topic of future trends has a lot of scope for your speaking expertise, as everything evolves so fast these days. This topic applies to areas as diverse as the future of technology, sales, health, or whatever area your audience is concerned with.

To succeed as a keynote speaker, complacency is not an option. You don't just write a keynote in the year 2000, and then for the next 16 years deliver that same keynote. Your message will need to constantly evolve with changing times and circumstances. Staying on top of your field will require a constant supply of resilience, creativity and an informed eye on future trends!

5. Pay to speak

This option applies in particular to platform selling, and multi-speaker events where you'll share the stage with a number of different speakers. These events are often run by promoters who will ask you to pay for the privilege of being on their stage. You will, however, benefit from the fact that they have a massive marketing machine, so they're able to put hundreds or even thousands of people into the room for you.

Remember that even though you pay for such speaking gigs, it's also an opportunity to sell, so you could make your money back on your upfront investment.

6. Sponsored speaking

Question: what can you do if you're really good at speaking, but you don't actually have a subject yourself, don't have a business, don't offer any services or have anything that you can sell at the back-end after and during your speaking? Answer: become a sponsored speaker!

There are a lot of charities out there and associations who pay speakers to deliver content on their behalf. There are also other opportunities, if you look hard enough. A funny example is Pfizer. If you're really passionate about Viagra, you could perhaps approach them because they will pay you hundreds of thousands of pounds (or dollars) for your ability to deliver their content to different pharmaceutical conferences. There's a lot of money to be made in this field.

7. Speaker training

Training companies like Speaker Express are looking for facilitators and trainers as well as speakers. You can put your speaking skills to use by training others to get better.

Being a trainer is a good way to get yourself out there and shape your speaking skills through practice. If not training speakers, running training in another area of your work (e.g. sales training) is also a form of speaking that will give you experience in front of an audience and managing a room.

If you are keen on this option, we're always on the lookout for people who can authentically connect with an audience, as are other training companies so just get in touch with the managing directors to express your interest.

8. MCing / hosting events

MCing or hosting events is very different from being a speaker because as an MC you glue the entire event together. As an MC/host, you need to understand flow, audience energy management and have a commanding personality, because you're the one raising the energy for all the speakers at the event.

At Speaker Express, one of the modules in our speaking accelerator focuses on MC training, which helps you as a speaker but also enables you to step further into your power. We then give our members the opportunity to MC our club nights, so they can gain live experience in front of an audience.

Don't underestimate the undertaking of MCing, it's a tough job and better suited to some than others. It takes an organised mind and ability to stay present and flexible. If you think it's for you, start by hosting small events and build yourself up to bigger ones. Hosting conferences can pay very well and some make a career out of this alone.

9. Speaking to sell

This is when your whole presentation is geared towards leading the audience to buy from you. While doing the presentation, you add value and demonstrate your unique solution to the audience's problem and continuously re-enforce that you have the solution. This is a very common use of speaking. When it is done right, and to the right audiences, it massively accelerates the growth of your business, brand awareness and cash flow. Often multi-speaker events follow this format which is very common in the personal development industry.

How to set your fee

Here is a formula you can use to work out your fee:

(Note that the figures have been chosen to keep it simple. You can eliminate those numbers and replace them with your own).

Day rate + design time + potential earnings (if you can't sell) = fee

Let's say (for the sake of simplicity) that your day rate is £500 (or Euros, Dollars, or whatever your local currency may be).

Imagine it takes you one day to rejig your talk for the day. That's another £500.

Then, there is potential earning that you won't make because you are not up-selling from your talk, which needs to be compensated for. This is the amount you might normally bring in sales (if you weren't being paid to speak) – let's imagine this is £3,000.

£500 + £500 + £3,000 = £4,000

This is your speaker fee if you are **not selling** at the event. Travel is on top of that and/or any expenses. None of this is set in stone and depends on the event, you may need to be flexible with your fee and adapt it to the event organiser's budget.

Remember that earnings will not always come from being paid to speak; sometimes money will come from being on stage and then gaining leads that will convert into sales later, which means of course the potential earnings are much higher. We know people who got paid a few hundred to speak and then went on to make thousands, or even millions, following connections made at that event.

We always get asked, "What is the bare minimum to ask for?" I always say to start at £1000. However, if you are new, then ask for whatever you feel comfortable charging. The formula above will help with that.

Sometimes, money comes from simply getting on stage and the profile that it enhances. Use your gut here. Sometimes, if the audience is your ideal target market and a great opportunity for you to promote your brand, it may be worth charging less.

Always remember that when it comes to monetising your speaking, it starts inside with your beliefs; then, it is how you add value to an audience and the results they will get by listening to you. Charge your worth and keep sharing your 'cure'.

Harriet's Story: From free to fee

Let's look at a real-life example of how you go from free to fee. Well-being coach, Harriet, completed her coaching diploma. Her background was in the finance industry. Harriet was a very skilled coach with many hours of 1-on-1 coaching under her belt when she started considering speaking.

When she met us in 2014, we were running a training called 'Speak Without Limits' and years later Harriet said to us: "When I realised I would have to speak at the training, I felt sick to my stomach and nearly threw up on the hotel carpet." She was very close to leaving the room, yet something made her stay. She refused to give in to the fear, nerves and voice in her head. She stuck it out.

As a result, she is now a powerful example of what can happen when your courage overrides all internal fears. Once she finished the 'Speak Without Limits' training, she knew that was her path and joined our 6-month training programme. Harriet showed up to every training, worked hard and applied what she had learned. She became one of the most sought-after speakers in the UK, sold out many of her talks at lightning speed, got signed by an agent and took her business to a whole new level. She is also now seen as much more than a coach; she is seen as a thought-leader and a voice in inspiring women in the entrepreneurial and corporate world. An incredible journey.

Harriet's example shows that when starting out speaking, it's not necessarily the order of what to learn first – it's about the implementation and taking your learnings from the training room into the real world. Today, most of Harriet's VIP coaching clients have been attracted to work with her because of seeing her speak on various stages. Harriet speaks on different stages in the personal development, corporate and educational sectors.

She has become one of the most highly-rated speakers at the world's biggest personal development Meetup – Interesting Talks, London. We will talk about how easy it is to get speaking gigs later by following the right sequence and putting the hours in.

The more Harriet spoke beyond the training room, the better she became and started to get paid directly for speaking, rather than just using speaking as a marketing tool for her coaching business.

The positive financial effect of speaking on your business is still something not enough businesses tap into and it can be one of the best investments ever made, as the opportunities are endless when it comes to raising your profile.

At the time of writing this book, Harriet just completed a European tour for an investment company and was just about to sign with a second speaker bureau.

Here are 3 key things that enabled Harriet to go from feeling sick at the thought of speaking to being signed by an agent:

1. Focus
    When signing up for a training programme, prioritise to implement what you learn. Harriet didn't get distracted nor did she sign up for any other programmes whilst focusing on her speaking.

2. Relationships
    If you aren't yet, become really good at making connections. It's one of the things that came naturally to Harriet. She started sending a number of potential clients our way. Have a guess what that did? Whenever someone was looking for a speaker, we thought of Harriet first as we

wanted to return the favour. I also know a number of other speakers who are registered with the same bureau as Harriet. But she tops everyone in number of bookings and I am convinced it's because she's bringing additional business to her bureau.

3. Consistency

    Before every speaking gig, Harriet does a Facebook Live. We have known her for many years now and those Lives never fail. She simply says something like: "Hey it's Harriet, I am here at another sold-out talk for Funzing (www.funzing.com) and tonight I will be talking about 'The Secrets to Emotional Wellbeing'..." This shows her followers what she is up to, but also creates a level of curiosity and has ensured her additional bookings.

A suggested pitch flow to follow

I have said this before and I will say it again, from the moment you step in front of people, you are selling. Selling yourself, your brand, your service or products – maybe all of them, maybe one of them. The truth is you are always selling.

To sell with respect to your audience and your potential customer, that is what needs to be considered. To do that, here is a proven flow to follow when you get to the pitch part of your presentation.

1. **Gain permission** to sell. We do this to make sure you have opened people up to being sold to. While the whole talk is often an indirect pitch, we don't want the audience to be too shocked when the talk shifts focus into a call-to-action/pitch. Signal the shift in focus and get their 'buy-in' by saying something like *"Is it OK if I tell you how we can carry on working together?"*

2. **Re-earn the right.** As per signature talk, when you are entering the pitch section of your talk you have to remind

the audience why you have been speaking about the topic and what has given you the right to do it.

3. **Reiterate the problem and create urgency**. Once you have reminded them of your credibility it is important to remind the audience of the problem and the importance of addressing it. For example, you could use a thought-provoking question or shocking stat to get your audience to think about the importance of addressing it.

4. **Remind the audience of your methodology.** Throughout your talk you must have added value and educated the audience enough that even if they walk away and don't work with you, they got something great from seeing you talk. There's nothing worse than only being sold to without feeling that you got value. During the pitch, remind the audience of your system, process or methodology that solves the problem.

5. Show **case studies/success stories.** Demonstrate people who came to you with a problem and how they used the methodology to get where they are today; demonstrate results they achieved.

6. **Show options**: 2-3 price points, explain each option, if you show 1 it is easier for people to say no! But 2 or 3 options with clear explanations gets people doing the maths and selecting which is best for them. Remember that too many options can get confusing, and a confused mind says no!

7. **Drop into a relevant story** to emphasise the importance of addressing the problem. Explain how your experience relates to what you're selling (why you do it) – drop into your heart space, connect to your 'why' and show people that you truly care.

8. If it's appropriate, **show the special offer**. Always make sure you explain why you are making a special offer, and how long the offer is on for.

9. **Next steps** – how do people sign up? Give a clear call to action and make it easy for people to sign up.

We have a Facebook group full of entrepreneurs who sell through speaking. In this group, the community talk all things pitching and selling through speaking. Join the group to explore more about this and how it is working in reality for other business owners. It's called **Entrepreneurs Who Sell Through Speaking.**

CHAPTER 11

The Speakers' Method: Build Profile

The sixth and final element of The Speakers' Method is all about how you build your profile. This all depends on the type of profile you want. One of our members owns four companies and wants to be seen as a thought leader in his industry, but he isn't concerned about social media or media exposure. He welcomes it, but doesn't focus on it. Other members we work with proactively seek to use both the old-school media (such as TV and radio) as well as new (social media) to raise their profile.

Building your profile can feel daunting at first, but quickly spirals into a positive loop. The more exposure you have, the higher your profile builds. The higher your profile, the more you will get booked and paid as a speaker. The more you are booked, the quicker your business will grow.

Four steps to visibility that every speaker can (and should) be taking

I often hear people say: "I've wasted years afraid of stepping up and being seen. I'm worried about not knowing enough or being found out for not being the expert." These are thoughts generated by the impostor syndrome.

Often – in life and in business – we take the 'safe' option: playing small, hiding, saying "no" when we should be saying "YES!" How safe is this approach, really? Because the last time I checked, playing safe led to limited exposure and limited income. Safe gets us nowhere.

We all have different ideas, and ideas have the power to change the world. But they must be communicated in a way that resonates with others, by someone who has the status of an expert and who the audience can trust.

The fastest way to build an audience is using social media. Here are four steps you can take:

1. Have a critical look at your social media. What do people see about you on your social media channels? How are you showing up? Do you post frequently enough for your audience? Would a speaker booker or conference organiser get the right impression? Does every post gain you more followers? Do at least some people engage with you and your content? Do people send you DMs (direct messages) about wanting to work with you?

2. Create a powerful build-up for your speaking engagements in the form of short stories on social media. So, for example, after clearly defining which online channel your target audience hangs out on, start with a post saying something like: "Amazing – just been booked to speak at XYZ. Here is the link, meet you there." Maybe add how you met the event organiser. Then, a couple of days before the gig, start to tease the content, e.g. "Did you know that 85% of new speakers struggle with getting speaking gigs? I mainly get my gigs through recommendations, but there are two additional strategies I use and I will share them with you at the event." Or post an image of one of your slides. You can also do that via Facebook live, Instagram stories or YouTube if you prefer videos. Remember to focus mainly on the medium your target audience is using. And lastly, before the event starts, do a short Facebook Live along the lines of: "Hey, I just arrived at xyz. The event is sold out and I can't wait to share my tips on xyz." Or do a Facebook Live afterwards getting one of the attendees to share their insights. Get creative. There are so many options to increase your social media visibility.

3. "That person has a PR rep so of course she gets gigs." "He faced a life-or-death situation so has something valuable to talk about." "She just got lucky." Recognise any of these *extremely limiting thoughts*? I thought you might. When we try to convince ourselves that others are luckier, more special, more connected, more qualified, we hold ourselves in a place of inaction and back from the success that would be ours. Stop dreaming about what you could achieve if only you had a PR team, unlimited budget,10,000 followers on Instagram, etc., and commit, and – here's the key – be consistent with it. It could be a weekly Facebook Live, a monthly newsletter, daily Instagram posts with valuable content, or monthly events like we've run at Speaker Express consistently every month since 2011. That's how you progress. Commit. Measure. If it's not bringing you more visibility or results, ditch it and amend your strategy.

4. Make sure that after every talk, you walk away with assets to enhance your profile:
   - Testimonials of you and your product.
   - Great Images of you speaking.
   - Little bite-size videos.
   - Another speaking gig.
   - A write-up about your talk.

Long-term consistency trumps short-term intensity. That's how the world works: the most successful people are long-term thinkers with a clear strategy. Decide on your branding, your business/speaker vision and then come back to the present and do the things you have to do to achieve your goal.

To get our free booklet on visibility as a speaker go to:
https://tinyurl.com/Spgvisibilty
Password: nottinghillspeaker

CHAPTER 12

The Origin of
The Speakers' Method

Over the years, Annik and I have attended many different trainings relating to public speaking. Some people train you to be robots – to "stand here" and "put your arm there" etc. – and have their own way of training. Others focus on how to structure a presentation (often without actually presenting it).

In our experience, a one-size-fits-all mentality does not work. We find that it is more about discovering what works for you and the teacher that resonates with you the best. Over time, as we built the business, we found that The Speakers' Method is our preferred methodology and captures everything you are likely to need.

When we asked our members what they got out of the training, most members mentioned some, if not all, of the areas included in our methodology. One day, Annik and I sat in my house in Surrey in the UK, and started to itemise everything we did. We sat there for hours looking for a captivating name that in three magical words would capture everything we do.

There were four of us in my living room, throwing around all kinds of names, but none stuck or felt right. We all reached that point of frustration and it was time to get some air and take a break. I got up and offered to pop to the shop to grab some tasty peri peri chicken. We sat there eating away, talking about how good the chicken was and other random things when my good friend, Rich Clayton, a branding specialist who was leading us throughout the day suddenly stopped, dropped his chicken (which was a big moment – no one drops their chicken when it is that good) and said: "The Speakers' Method!" There was stunned silence. Everyone put down their chicken. We all looked at each other, hesitating.

He said it again, "The Speakers' Method". We looked at each other again and no one needed to say anything else. We all knew that was it – it captured everything we do. It was the system we had been teaching and now, finally, we had a name for it. Life was never the same after that...

Gradually, over time, we have honed The Speakers' Method to be a slick impactful methodology which has supported thousands of speakers worldwide.

Throughout this book, you have read case studies of people we have worked with at different levels, using our system to achieve great results. We should point out though, that there is no magic pill and no overnight success. To be world class, you have to train and work world class – which means investing, applying what you learn, practising, getting out there, self-promoting, knowing your value and never ever forgetting the basics. It means remaining grounded, humble, being of service to your cause and *consistent*.

One way to remain consistent is to learn and apply The Speakers' Method – continuously improving, honing and training towards massive impact for you and your business. Part of the reason we brought all our training modules together into The Speakers' Method is to show the importance of all elements. Each of the modules works in conjunction with each other. This is also why we offer our training as a programme covering all six areas, to ensure that speakers are working on their speaking strategy holistically, which is how the results are really obtained.

PART THREE:
Inspiration and Implementation

CHAPTER 13

Our Brand Story

As I've talked a lot about brand stories, I thought I would share ours, along with a few business lessons we have learnt along the way.

It starts with Annik's story, and as with most entrepreneurs' beginnings, a problem she experienced and wanted to solve. Wanting to overcome her fear of public speaking, she would attend trainings but then become very frustrated that once the training was over, there was no environment where she could go to practise on a regular basis. She recognised the importance of regular practice and feedback in the pursuit of becoming an accomplished speaker, and that's where the idea of creating a space for speakers came from.

The idea was simple – once a month, budding speakers get together to practise their talks and get feedback from judges. The judges are professional speakers who are ahead of the trainees. Annik set about getting this going; she found a venue and put out the word to her network. She enrolled me into her vision, we put together a structure and the first club night was delivered.

Looking back, it was a lot of fun.

From idea to execution

There was a lot of work to do to turn this into a sustainable concept and at the time I was running one of my other businesses, so Annik took charge. Picture this: Annik was promoting this event herself in between her other job, contacting people by email, Facebook, calling them in any way possible to get them to attend, creating a buzz about it.

Then, the big night arrived: our first club night.

Imagine red carpets, a queue outside, a big room in a fancy venue with a full audience, photographer snapping us as we walked along. It was amazing … and untrue!

Here is what it really looked like. You enter a dingy pub in Kentish Town, walk down the creaking stairs and feel the sticky floor under your feet. At the bottom of the stairs is a very dark room with black walls and just two light bulbs hanging down, and old sagging sofas to sit on. In reality the walk down the stairs felt more like a journey to a horror movie set than a Speakers' Club night.

However, the night went brilliantly! Despite the strange smell, darkness and sticky floor, people had a great time.

While the venue had an 'arty' feel, we both agreed that it wasn't the place or image for the brand we wanted to build. We agreed we had to use venues with a little bit more class, and it's safe to say we never set foot in that dingy little pub again.

'The Pony' was born

The club night became a monthly event and was gathering momentum, but it needed a name, it needed an identity. Annik being the creative person that she is, announced her idea to name us 'Pony Express Speakers' Club'. The Wild West story about the Pony Express is a great metaphor for public speaking:

The Pony Express is one of the most colourful episodes in American history, one which can be used to measure not only the growth of the nation, but the pioneering spirit of our predecessors. The name "Pony Express" evokes images of courageous young men crossing long stretches of country, frequently under harsh conditions, facing the constant threat of death like so many legendary events of the 'Old Wild West'.

She explained to me: "It's like public speaking – it can feel like you are risking your life to deliver a message!" Very clever, so now we had a name and a night, and that's how an idea moved from Annik's head into becoming something very real.

From the very beginning, I could see there was something much bigger to this, something that would have longevity and could become a viable business. It took almost three years for Annik to come around and accept that idea. Being fired twice from her sales job helped to convince her. The first three years of Speaker Express (or Pony Express Speakers' Club as it was then) were dabbling years, a hobby business. Then once Annik made up her mind to make it into a business, and invested into it full time, we grew fast.

One area in which we were successful throughout the first three years was building the brand and reputation. As we had done this well and created a loyal community, the transition wasn't a hard one. Remember: as a speaker, you are also a brand. It is important you treat yourself as a brand and when you use public speaking as a tool, you are representing your company brand which means that everything counts.

Stepping into the limelight

We hit an interesting moment in our positioning a few years ago, when Annik, although being one of the founders, was still hiding behind event running. At our public events she would be straightening the chairs, doing registrations and basically avoiding doing any public speaking! She would be hiding behind my ability to speak and sell. I had enough, as really Annik was the face of the brand, she was the one doing a lot of the promotional work and putting in the effort, yet she was busy avoiding being the front person. Not on my watch!

After a while, I called her out on it: "Annik, this is your vision, your concept and people see you as the face of the brand. Now get yourself in front of everyone and open the night, do the sales, and close the night." It's safe to say that ever since then Annik has been the face of the brand and has been speaking at pretty much all the club nights. Sometimes we all need a bit of tough love, don't we?

I am only too aware how easy it is to hide behind the business, how easy it is to avoid putting yourself out there. The rewards when you do use public speaking are awesome: your company is elevated, you get invited to industry events as an expert, you get to travel, and your business grows as a result.

Maybe you also need an "Elliot" to call you out and give you a bit of a kicking? It's no coincidence that Annik now speaks once a week on average, gets paid to do it and we have a thriving business which positively impacts other people's businesses. Imagine if she hadn't stepped forward and had always stayed hidden? Ask yourself – where in your business are you hiding? Or where could you add more stage time to your business?

Getting strategic

When Speaker Express started to grow up (i.e. become a profitable business), we had a lot of work to do internally. We had to ask questions such as:

- What are our individual roles?
- How are we going to create continuous cash flow?
- What is our customer's journey?
- What products do we need?
- Who is our ideal customer?
- What is our sales strategy / marketing strategy?

None of these questions were answered immediately, however those were the ones we urgently needed to address. We started to have weekly strategy sessions and set out to build the speakers' journey when they enrolled to work with us; we named the courses, the events and built our sales funnels.

After every club night, we would debrief:

- What worked?
- What didn't work?
- What would we do better?
- How many sales did we get?

Never stop refining and innovating

We tested different products and pricing. Looking back, I can't believe some of the pricing we gave for our six-month training programmes at the beginning. Crazy! If you heard that today, you would think either that we are a cheap brand, or something is wrong with us. But we learnt many lessons along the way, and discovered our values that have always stuck. Through all our changes, we have always been customer focused: we want to give massive value and for the people who we work with to have an amazing experience. This hasn't changed since the day we started.

We must have tried and tested 100 different structures until we reached the slick, winning one we have today. It's the same with our events – we did hundreds till we got the right format and it's the same with our trainings and memberships. We are always looking to do better.

It took until 2017 to formulate The Speakers' Method and that was a key moment with our brand.

Another aspect to growing this business is to move with your clients, grow and evolve. For a while, I knew that the name Pony Express Speaker Club was a cute name, and it had a great reputation, but it wouldn't appeal to the CEOs, the entrepreneurs, or business owners.

If you consider that we had spent seven years building up the Pony Express name and brand, you can understand Annik's hesitation to change everything. But like anything in business, it had to be done. We called in an international business advisor to help us not only change the name, but also solidify our sales strategy. After that meeting, Speaker Express was born. The pony was dead, and we never looked back.

Forming partnerships

One aspect that we have always believed in and enforced are partnerships. As I had built a business before getting involved with Speaker Express, I wanted to bring over successful strategies I had experienced before. One of them was to see how we could maximize on partnerships. Partnerships are one of the best ways to grow and accelerate business growth.

> *Organisations with different offerings for a similar market create a win-win.*

In our early years, I managed to arrange a venue where we could hold a club night every month for a year: they would provide the venue at no cost and in return they would pitch their membership to people attending. This is a formula that has worked for us throughout the years. As you can imagine, it saves us a lot of money, as well as giving us a base in central London which people love.

Strong partnerships with a mutual aim, benefit both parties and accelerate growth for both.

For example, recently we teamed up with the Institute of Directors in Mayfair, London, who provide us with rooms for our club nights and trainings. In return, they get people to sign up to their membership, so everyone is happy. This enables us to tell potential new clients that we are based in Mayfair and host our trainings at a grand venue for very low cost.

We have teamed up with another training company who support entrepreneurs on growing their business. They do teach them pitching; however, they don't teach them all about public speaking which is where we come in. On the reverse, we send them entrepreneurs who want to grow their businesses. For them, it cuts out marketing and gives them warm leads. Another big win.

CHAPTER 14

Success Principles

We've covered the methods and tools to use in order to get you speaking. Now I want to support you in implementing this into your business. Forming the spine of all of our trainings are 8 'Impact Principles' we developed over the years. From doing exit interviews with clients at the end of their time as part of the Speaker Express programs, these were the elements that stuck with them. Together, these principles formulate an attitude to speaking. Adopt this attitude and way of thinking, and you are sure to succeed.

1. Stage Time – Of Course!

Say yes to every opportunity. Someone invites you to speak, offers you their stage or looks for a volunteer in the audience – your answer is always "of course". Someone calls you because they are sick and want you to step in, say, "of course". Take every chance – drop every fear. As you get more and more experience, check in with the Fee Free Flee.

2. Dare to Bomb

We often learn more from failure than success. Be afraid of not giving it a go, not of getting things wrong. Progress over perfection. Feedback is never personal anyway – performance, feedback, revision, embrace it at all times, look for lessons and learn from them to move forward. It's your chance to go from good to great.

3. It's Not About Me

Once you realise you are on stage to be of service and not to let your crazy voices get in the way, your nerves will transform.

When your focus is on your audience, nerves will dissipate as the focus is not on what they will think about you but how you solve their problems. This concept is all about 'falling from your head into your heart'. When serving your customers/audience is your main focus, your business will grow the most.

4. With Vulnerability Comes Power

A lot of times we feel we must wear a mask when we speak. While we must come across with certainty and professionalism, adding vulnerability actually can make you more powerful. I have seen this with people who have pitched for millions and people who have shown they are vulnerable in order to empower an audience. Done right it wins every time. You may have heard of Brené Brown and her insights on vulnerability being the most accurate measurement of courage? If you haven't, please check her out. She reminds us that our imperfections are marks of authenticity and that's the beauty of humanity. Let yourself be seen. Be you.

5. The 3 Most Dangerous Words: "I KNOW THAT."

Our mind is like a parachute, it works best when open! Don't let your 'knowing' something stop you from hearing it again – knowing versus owning. Bite your tongue and be open.

6. Always Play at 111%

Dare to go too far! Playing small means you're comfortable, but not memorable. Greatness doesn't come from playing small. Do you play at 100% or more? Nerves are a sign that you are playing a bigger game – enjoy the ride! We love this special attitude when you think: 'I can't do this…' but then remind yourself, '…but I am doing it anyway!'

7. Repetition Creates Mastery

Practise and train. Be on top of your market. Watch other speakers. Be hungry for coaching. Practise and train some more.

8. Take Responsibility and Track your Progress

There are only two options: making progress or making excuses. If the opportunity doesn't exist, create it! Your success depends on what you put in. Review your goals and progress weekly. Spend 20 minutes reflecting and creating action steps. Ensure you look back and see how far you have come! Use your special notebook on a weekly basis. Be on top of your market. What do other speakers do? Develop original content to stand out and become the best you can be. Watch other speakers as often as possible. What can you do better in your own performance? Take 100% responsibility for your progress and results by taking action consistently. Be on time and lead by example so you can empower others.

Implementing your vision

No matter how slow you think you progress, you are still overtaking everybody on the couch.

Why do some people get ahead, even in busy times, and others do not? Here is the Secret:

Consistent, small steps are more likely to change habits than big leaps. Creativity and innovation are important, we agree 100%, but true discipline is the master of your success in the long-term.

Let's bring some more clarity to this concept and how to implement it on a yearly, monthly, weekly and daily basis.

Having a clear vision for your speaking as a strategy focuses your mind, simply because you know what is important and daily steps keep you on track. Your consistency is crucial and the separating factor between great and average.

Before setting your goals, you have to understand the following:

Milestones

Milestones are performance markers. The minimum effort to put into your goal/project/idea/business. For example: reading 5 pages daily, speaking once a month or writing 500 words a day.

Self-Doubt – Focus – VISION

It can be easy to panic when you see how others seem to get ahead in the race and you are not moving. Self-doubt may surface and make you feel that others are getting ahead faster and doing a better job. This can cause us to potentially get distracted by 'shiny little opportunities' which are not part of your vision and weaken your focus. Make corrections, if needed, but remind yourself of your vision daily and keep racing towards it.

TIP: FOCUS on one goal at the time!

From the heart

Your success should be based on your values – not external, delusional forces. Take time out to think and formulate your strategy. The resulting goals MUST be based on your values, your personality and working style. Check in with yourself: are the goals dictated by your head and external perception of you or do they come straight from within your heart?

Timeline – long enough to manage, yet short enough to have teeth

Strategising your outcomes must be right for your flow of work. Your timeline shouldn't be too short, as then you might be exposed to things out of your control (this can just be a simple flu). If your strategic timeline is too long it will lose its power.

Consistency

Sometimes you will be tired, but by progressing slowly (even with only little daily investment of 5 minutes) you are still overtaking everybody on the couch, come rain, shine, snow or wind. This way you will finish your keynote speech, your product, website or book faster than anyone who just keeps talking about what they want to achieve.

TIP: Whatever your circumstances, prove to yourself that results are not determined by any external conditions, but by your own actions! This really builds your confidence. Especially in today's fast-changing world – how many people really have the discipline and commitment to stick to something for a period of time?

Don't panic during rough times, that's where your vision is important and don't get arrogant during times of success. Stay consistent and resist short-term temptations if they are not part of your bigger picture. 'Lean' on your Speaker Express community to move forward. Learn from others – have an accountability buddy or join one of the masterminds. There will always be tough times. Never blame your circumstances, never blame others.

> *SHOW UP – PUSH THROUGH – STAY COMMITED AND NEVER GIVE UP!*

CHAPTER 15

Taking Consistent Action #tca

If you made it to the last chapter: KUDOS! You may have heard some of these steps before and think you know them, but it's all about the *application*.

Progress over perfection

I am often asked: "When is the right time to start or take your speaking to the next level?" My response is, "The time is always now." I always say, "Start before you are ready." As an entrepreneur, you will know this already (I hope). Remember no one can do this for you and there will always be another excuse to wait or hold off. Please don't: the rewards are only reaped after the seed is watered. Don't wait for the right time or for the opportunity to find you. Make it happen.

If you are willing to put in the hours, then you will always get a return on your investment. It can start with one simple action: attending an introductory training, or simply sitting down and writing out some content for a talk, and grow from there.

Something else I get asked a lot about is timelines: how long does it take? The truth is timelines vary. We have seen people get results within one month of working with us. We have also seen people who take longer. How quickly you want to achieve your goals is up to you. Those who show up to all the training, who apply everything we teach, are the ones who get the results fastest.

Consistency trumps perfection

Firstly, perfection is an illusion. Secondly, it is an excuse to avoid taking action, or releasing something. By being consistent, by starting before you are ready, you will surprise not only yourself but others as well. By doing the same talk time and time again, refining and improving it, results will start to roll in. By starting with 10 minutes and slowly growing your talk to 15 minutes, 30 minutes, and then one hour, the results will increase. The important part is being consistent.

We've compiled some tips to help you:

- Spend 30 minutes a day connecting with people you want to speak for.
- Practise your talk – even when you don't have any bookings – 3 times a week.
- Get mentoring and training on a monthly basis.
- Once a week, buy lunch for someone who can be a potential partner/supporter of yours.
- Post on social media consistently in a way that gets you invited to speak.
- Dare to have an opinion and share it.
- Produce content to draw in people who can invite you to speak.

These are examples of what it takes to be consistently seen, get booked and grow your brand, your company and make an impact through public speaking. Are you ready? Make your first call to get booked now! When you have your first booking jump on the Facebook page @speakerexpress – we would love to hear from you.

If you are a business owner or entrepreneur, you will be aware that competition for customers is fierce within most industries, both online and offline. Everyone is competing for that space in our brain to be the go-to person and/or brand. Branding is the key to differentiating yourself from the competition and one way to stand out is to consistently deliver talks that are engaging, educational and lead people to buy into your brand and company promise.

Everything counts

How you dress, the language you use, the slides – it must all be consistent when you get on stage, from a brand messaging point of view.

Once, I had to hold some training for a start-up in the tech space. They were going to pitch in Barcelona and had never really done any big-scale pitching in front of so many investors before, so we were going in to run some training with their team. When we received the brief, we were told, "I know you like to wear suits – don't! They won't trust you!" We were able to remain on brand because of our slides and messaging on the day. I wore a shirt with jeans and trainers; winning the trust and still managing to keep up appearances.

Consistency is the key to successful branding and positioning, and by speaking consistently it can accelerate the brand's reach. Remember that everything counts. Consistency goes beyond just standing up and speaking.

Can this really work for me?

Throughout the book I have shared various ways to use speaking to grow your business, from our very own Speakers' Method, to how to utilise it as a communication tool. Speaking is one of the most rewarding ways to not only grow your business but also to grow as a person.

"Can Speaker Express really help me get over the obstacles and be able to go that raw on stage?" This was the question that Lathi Dube asked us before deep diving into our trainings. The answer was "yes". What we needed to do in her case was to break down the obstacles into small bite-size chunks, and slowly move her through the stages of The Speakers' Method. Since doing that, she is now delivering authentic talks to big audiences regularly and making a name for herself.

Coming from a debt and corporate recovery background, Ron Mookerjee came to us as he was looking for a different way to get his message across to the audience. Working in this industry can be very challenging as it involves taking several difficult decisions and steps. He had great stories to share which had influenced him to shape his career as well as help him grow as a person. Ron came along to Speaker Express, where we helped to groom his public speaking abilities and brought out the best in him. While working with us, Ron improved and developed his public speaking skills.

As a result of Ron attending our course, we managed to boost his confidence, turning him into an awe-inspiring storyteller attracting the attention of everyone in the audience with his interesting thoughts and experiences, relating to others going through a similar journey.

> *No matter what your industry or background, if you have the desire to make a dent through public speaking, you can.*

Before you know it, you will be charging thousands for your time to speak, while generating a stream of new clients who will become your raving fans.

If you want more help from us to achieve that, you can look at our website for additional resources, and we would love you to share your learnings or results with us at @speakerexpress on Facebook or Instagram.

You can also do our free online assessment to get a clear indication of where you are as a speaker https://www.speakerexpress.co.uk/scorecard/

> *Go forward. Use your voice for good. Become an authority in your industry. Disrupt, jolt and shake them up.*

Printed in Poland
by Amazon Fulfillment
Poland Sp. z o.o., Wrocław

61544709R00082